MW01130233

WILLIAM L. COLEMAN

Fins, Feathers, and Faith

BETHANY BACKYARD®

MINNEAPOLIS, MN 55438

Published by Bethany House Publishers
A Ministry of Bethany Fellowship International
11400 Hampshire Avenue South
Bloomington, Minnesota 55438
www.bethanyhouse.com

Printed in the United States of America by Bethany Press International, Bloomington, Minnesota 55438

Library of Congress Cataloging-in-Publication Data

Coleman, William L.
    [Listen to the animals]
    Fins, feathers, and faith : wisdom from God's amazing creation / by William L. Coleman ; illustrated by Chris Wold Dyrud
        p. cm.
Originally published: Listen to the animals. Minneapolis : Bethany Fellowship, © 1979.
        ISBN 0–7642–2461–1
    1. Christian children—Religious life—Juvenile literature. 2. Christian children—Conduct of life—Juvenile literature. 3. Animals—Religious aspects—Christianity—Juvenile literature.
[1. Animals—Religious aspects—Christianity. 2. Christian life. 3. Prayer books and devotions.]
I. Dyrud, Chris Wold, Ill. II. Title.
    BV4571.3 .C65 2001
    242'.62—dc21

                                      00-012156

Dedicated to
North Shores Baptist Church
St. Clair Shores, Michigan

Acknowledgment

Jim Coleman played a big part in putting this book together. His help in research and reading copy are greatly appreciated.

WILLIAM L. COLEMAN has been a prolific author for many years. This is his fifth nature book. He has written for children, teens, and adults.

Books by William Coleman
from Bethany House Publishers

Contents

God Made an Amazing World

God made an octopus that can eat its own arm and grow another one. Some insects sleep for seventeen years and know just when to wake up. A cheetah cat can run seventy miles an hour. These are just a small part of our Creator's great imagination.

When Jesus Christ taught, He used fish, lilies, sparrows, and foxes to help us remember. When Paul wrote about anger, he reminded us of the sun. Ezekiel called the Pharaoh a bubbling crocodile.

In this short book, we use the Bible and nature to teach about God, ourselves, our feelings, and our friends.

Enjoy it and grow.

William L. Coleman
Aurora, Nebraska

1

MAIN ATTRACTION

Where is the crowd at the zoo? On most Saturday afternoons children are probably packed around the monkey cage. These cute animals often put on the best fun in any town.

Some of the most popular monkeys in the zoo are rhesus (pronounced *REE-sus*) monkeys. They come from the jungles of India and are in almost no danger of becoming extinct. They are like noisy bees in the wild.

Noisy is the right word to describe them. Rhesus monkeys will jump, fight, argue, chatter, and swing. That is why the crowd is usually watching them.

They have large families and evidently love to argue with each other. But they don't stay angry. After a string of harsh chatter and some fast action, they calm down and become friends again. In a few minutes they are picking bugs off each other like good buddies.

Most monkeys are afraid of water. Not the rhesus. Give one a small pond and it looks like a champion swimmer.

If you study monkeys closely, you can soon tell one type from another. The proboscis (*pro-BOSS-iss*) monkey is easy to pick out. Its nose sticks out like a large flat thumb and hangs down to its chin.

The only place proboscis monkeys live is in Borneo. They don't seem to do well in zoos, so most children won't get to see them.

We are more likely to see spider monkeys. They get their name from long, thin arms and a full tail. There is practically no meat on these

creatures. The fur makes them look well rounded, but don't be fooled. Underneath they are skinny creatures.

If spider monkeys had their way, they would always stay in the trees. Swinging from limb to limb is their idea of living. Swinging from their tails and picking fruit with their hands and feet keeps them happy all day.

If you are lonely, you might think about buying a howler monkey. Not only do they like to talk, but they do it so loudly you might wonder if the house is falling in. Their sound is something like an automobile horn. Imagine yourself in a room with this thing going off continuously.

Just listening, you might think the howler monkey is being attacked. Actually, he is just making a great deal of unnecessary noise.

Sometimes people talk the same way a howler monkey does. We often talk too much. Even worse, we say things that get others upset for nothing. If we say good things about people, talking is helpful like medicine. But when we merely chatter and don't think, we might really hurt someone's feelings.

You are supposed to be a wise man, and yet you give us all this foolish talk. You are nothing but a windbag. It isn't right to speak so foolishly. What good do such words do?

Job 15:2–3 (TLB)

1. Which monkey likes to swim?
2. Where do spider monkeys like to stay?
3. How can we stop from saying cruel things about others?

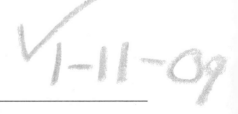

GUARD OUR LIPS.

2

THE PINCUSHION

The porcupine is not a large animal, but it is feared by some of the biggest. Even a tiger will think twice before tangling with this two-foot-long terror.

Most of the time this prickly pincushion merely minds its own business. But if something wants to start trouble, "Porky" will give it a fight.

From its neck to its tail is a heavy coat of quills that look like knitting needles. Each quill is sharp and painful if it sticks you.

Porcupines seem to be slow and helpless. Yet, if you attack one, it will turn quickly and try to back into you. It is so fast that it will probably get its attacker by surprise. Sometimes dogs will run at a porcupine, expecting an easy dinner. Porky will turn, lift its tail, and push its back at the rushing dog. The quills stick into the dog's face and come loose from the porcupine. The dog limps away with a painful howl. Some quills are fifteen inches long and sink deep into the skin.

A few stories about porcupines aren't true. They can't really shoot their quills like arrows. But they can push their body fast enough to cause serious injury.

A porcupine has thirty thousand quills on its back and sides. Don't try to count them, or Porky might give a few to you. But that would be no problem since Porky would quickly grow them back.

A quill is not merely a sharp stick. Each quill has tiny blades all over it. After it goes inside an animal, the quill will push itself deeper and deeper, even after it has left the porcupine. The result is often a nasty wound.

Mountain lions can successfully hunt porcupines. But even they have to be careful to attack only the head or belly. The lion must carefully and quickly roll the porcupine on its back.

A coyote that attacks a porcupine may get killed. When a coyote gets a face full of quills, the quills begin to work their way into the coyote's throat and head. It's not long before the wounded attacker is dead.

Usually, the animal that gets hurt by a porcupine is the one that doesn't look at the danger. It doesn't realize or care what the porcupine can do. It just rushes in and comes away the loser.

We often do the same thing. "Why not just try some foolish thing? What does it matter if we get into trouble?" Because we don't stop to think, we end up in more trouble than we ever imagined. A smart person stops to think it over. When he realizes the harm, he decides against trouble.

The wise see danger ahead and avoid it, but fools
keep going and get into trouble.
Proverbs 22:3 (NCV)

1. What does a quill do after it enters a body?
2. How does a porcupine attack?
3. Have you ever gotten into more trouble than you expected?

HELP US THINK BEFORE WE DO SOMETHING ME MIGHT BE SORRY FOR.

3

HIDING IN CHINA

We were sure they didn't exist. Travelers used to talk about a giant bear with black-and-white fur. Few people believed them. More than a hundred years ago a missionary sent a black-and-white fur to Paris, but people still didn't believe.

Finally, in 1937, a beautiful giant panda was captured, and today practically everyone has heard of them.

It is easy to understand why most people had never seen them. Giant pandas live in only one part of the world. They are found high in the mountains of China. But even in China, few people have seen giant pandas in the wild. They live such hidden lives that, for a long time, little was known about them.

The giant panda is an endangered species. They are generally picky eaters and feed mostly on bamboo shoots. Their favorite type of bamboo is found only in one part of China. If people move too far into their territory, pandas will be pushed onto poor land. The lack of food there could cut the number of giant pandas way down.

Giant pandas look loving and playful, but we shouldn't be fooled. Pandas don't like to be handled. One quick swipe of their sharp claws could do a great deal of damage.

Though often called one, the panda is not a bear. For one thing, pandas eat only vegetables—unlike the diet of bears, which includes meat. The panda is an animal like none other.

This rare animal was first captured for America by a woman named Mrs. Harkness. Her husband, Mr. Harkness, had planned to catch a panda for a zoo, but he died before he arrived in China. Mrs. Harkness, without any experience, decided to give it a try and brought the first one out of China.

A great many things are scarce in life. Expensive jewels, gold, and some animals are hard to find. The Bible tells us about something else that's rare. Sometimes a person will give his or her life for a friend or a relative. But almost never will a person die to save a bad person.

Jesus Christ did a rare thing. He knew you and I would be sinners, but still He died to pay for our sins. Christ is more rare than a panda or anything else. There can be only one Son of God. He did a most unusual thing in dying for us.

Very few people will die for someone else.
Although perhaps for a good man someone might
possibly die. But Christ died for us while we were
still sinners. In this way God shows us
his great love for us.

Romans 5:7–8 (ICB)

1. Where do pandas live?
2. How many giant pandas are left in the world?
3. Why did Christ die?

THANKS FOR LOVING SINNERS LIKE ME.

4

THE LONG NAP

There is an odd little insect that lives only in the eastern part of the United States. If you want to see it, you have to be in just the right place at the right time.

The cicada (pronounced *sih-KAY-da*) comes out of the ground once every seventeen years. If you miss it, move farther south. The cicadas there appear every thirteen years. But even if you get the correct year, you can't sit around. Cicadas live for only six weeks above the ground. If you miss them, you have a long wait coming.

During the few weeks above ground, cicadas have much to get done. When they come out, they are wrapped in a tight shell, like a jacket. Immediately, they start climbing something, such as a tree or a plant. They have an urge to go *up*.

The young cicada is looking for something to hold on to. When it settles down, the insect begins taking off its wrap. Usually, it takes an hour of hard struggle. Now the cicada is a strong adult that needs to make the most of its time.

The female starts laying eggs in the first week. Many of the cicadas die soon after. If they are to carry on, the eggs must find a safe place.

Female cicadas use a special blade on their tails to saw holes in tiny twigs. In each hole they put twenty-four to twenty-eight eggs. Each twig will have several holes or nests. One female will lay up to six hundred eggs.

In six weeks the eggs hatch, and the tiny cicadas crawl out. They fall directly to the ground and start digging in. Their home will be nearly two feet below the surface. They are looking for juicy roots to live on. For the next seventeen years the cicada will suck on these roots. They don't seem to do any damage to trees.

Birds eat many of the adult cicadas. Mites and other insects feed on the eggs. This helps to keep the cicada population in balance. Each group has forty thousand eggs, and they could easily get out of control.

The cicadas know when their seventeen-year nap is to finish. A few weeks before, they dig their way up toward the top. They sit there only one inch below the surface. Then some unknown signal comes, and they dig their way out.

Cicadas have some sort of unknown clock inside them. They don't come out during the wrong year. They don't complain and start up after two weeks. There is a safe time for everything, and they seem willing to wait.

Often our timing gets off. Adults try to act like children, and children want to be adults and drive cars too soon. Young people try to tell their parents what to do.

Life takes patience. When we are adults, we can make decisions we can't make now. Matches, machines, money, and marriage are usually better handled with experience and time.

There is a right time for everything.
Ecclesiastes 3:1 (TLB)

---

1. **Where do cicadas live?**
2. **How long do the adults live?**
3. **What would you like to do as an adult?**

TIME IS A BEAUTIFUL GIFT.

5

THE BEAUTIFUL JAGUAR

Don't ever get a jaguar mad at you. This huge cat has a terrible temper. It has been known to hunt armed men for days and then try to kill them.

Jaguars are the largest cats in Mexico. They are almost as big as tigers, weighing four hundred pounds. Their coats are a beautiful yellow with black spots. But don't let their beauty fool you. Jaguars are among the strongest hunters in nature.

There is one story told of a jaguar who killed a horse. He then dragged the dead animal for more than a mile.

The people of South and Central America aren't too happy with this talented cat. Every year it kills thousands of cattle and some people. If an area floods, a jaguar may roam into a village looking for dry land and food.

These cats aren't picky eaters. They like crocodiles, turtle eggs, and deer. They are also excellent fishermen. According to some stories, they will stand over a river and look into the water. Fish will come near to see what it is, then become a jaguar's dinner.

Jaguars are so dangerous in parts of Brazil that men are paid to hunt them. One man is particularly brave. He uses dogs to corner a four-hundred-pound jaguar. When the cat finally charges the hunter, he kills it with a simple spear. He has killed over 240 of them in this way.

In the world of nature, the jaguar has no enemies. There is no animal that can defeat this big cat. Only humans can effectively master it, and not always.

Jaguars are one of the few cats that like to swim. They are so good at it that they can push a dead cow into a river and then jump in themselves. Guiding it with its mouth, the jaguar can take its catch miles away.

Jaguars are just as much at home in a tree as they are on land or sea. They prefer to roam at night but do make some trips during the day.

The jaguar takes such good care of itself that it may live to be twenty years old. Each year the female gives birth to two or four cubs.

It is hard for people to enjoy the jaguar. Though it is beautiful, it doesn't mix well with people. Yet, if kept far from humans, jaguars play an important part in nature. They keep it balanced so there are not too many crocodiles, turtles, or even fish.

Every creature has its place in nature. Each person has his or her important role in life. Everything God has made is good if it is used correctly.

For everything God has created is good,
and nothing is to be rejected if it is
received with thanksgiving.

1 Timothy 4:4 (NIV)

1. How much does a jaguar weigh?
2. How did one hunter kill a jaguar?
3. Name two good reasons God has for using you.

THANKS FOR CALLING ME GOOD.

6

How Deep Is the Ocean?

Would you like to get into a specially built ship and travel to the deepest part of the ocean? Don't say yes too quickly. It is possible to make this trip, but it is terribly dangerous.

The deepest part of the ocean is believed to be near the Philippine Islands. The bottom of the sea, at that point, is seven miles, or 35,800 feet, beneath the surface.

In 1960, two men were courageous enough to take a submarine to the bottom. A normal submarine would have been crushed like a smashed soda can. The pressure at that depth is seven tons per square inch. The men had to build a special craft called a *bathyscaphe* (pronounced *BATH-ih-skafe*).

The men's names were Jaques Piccard and Don Walsh. They saw things that no man had ever seen before—and lived to tell about it. Their total stay was around fifteen minutes. The bathyscaphe started to squeak under the pressure, and they had to come up.

Now, many years later, no one else has gone to that depth again. So far, it is entirely too risky.

Will man ever walk on the ocean bottom at its deepest point? Almost anything is possible. Maybe someone reading this book will do it. But for now, it doesn't look likely. A protective suit strong enough for the job hasn't been made yet.

Today, ocean scientists rely strongly on machines and cameras at great depths. These stop just a few feet from the ocean floor and take pictures of fascinating creatures.

The sea is dark at this depth. It is so dark even the fish have to carry flashlights. It's true. Some fish have tiny lights on their foreheads like coal miner hats. It allows them to be seen by each other.

Fish adjust to the heavy pressure at seven miles beneath the surface. Their bodies are made of thin material. Some are so clear we can see through them.

Although the ocean is deep, it isn't silent. Microphones have picked up all sorts of chatter and clicking. Everything is buzzing some type of talk.

More than just an interesting place to study, the sea is where God began His creation. Peter tells us that our great God made the world out of the waters around us. Our faith in God can grow stronger when we look at the ocean floor He made. That amazing Creator is our personal heavenly Father.

But they deliberately forget that long ago by God's Word the heavens existed and the earth was formed out of water and by water.

2 Peter 3:5 (NIV)

1. How deep is the ocean at its deepest point?
2. Why don't people visit the ocean bottom more often?
3. What can the ocean floor remind us of?

THE SMALL FISH LIVING SEVEN MILES DEEP ARE PROOF OF THE GOOD HAND OF GOD.

7

LITTLE NIGHT CREATURES

Would you like to go on a bat hunt? Would you like to see them hanging upside down in a cave and sleeping in the daytime? It isn't difficult to do. There are over two thousand types of bats, and they live almost all over the world.

Before you start your search, there are a few facts to keep in mind. The best places to find them are in dark attics, abandoned mines, the roofs of barns, rotted trees, and of course, caves. If you find one, you will probably get a half dozen or more. They love to hang around in groups.

For those bold enough to look for bats at night, there is added help. Listen for a whistling sound like boiling water in a teakettle. A bat sends out these sounds to tell itself where it is. A bat depends on its ears to get around in the dark. Called a *sonar system*, the sound waves bounce off walls and rocks and guide the flying mammal. Bats are quick and can go great distances. Some travel eight hundred miles and return home again safely.

Bats are likely to eat anything. The little brown bats live on insects. The flying fox bats make a meal of fruit. Often they take only small bites from each fruit and ruin large crops. There is also the fish-eating bat. It snatches its food right out of the water. Long-nosed bats drink nectar from plants.

The most famous bat is the vampire bat—and it really does exist. They don't turn into people, but they do drink human blood.

Vampire bats are found from Mexico to Brazil. They have teeth as sharp as razors. Their choice food is animal blood, but they also attack people. The bat looks for a place on the body where it can get plenty of blood. It may select the ear lobe or tip of the nose.

The top layer of skin is opened painlessly. Often the victim won't even wake up. The vampire doesn't suck the blood but laps it up like a kitten drinking milk from a saucer. These bats drink blood until they feel stuffed. Some can barely fly when they are done.

The real danger of the vampire bat is not the amount of blood they take. Some people wake up completely unaware, except for the cut on their nose. The more serious problem is the diseases they carry. Bats may have the dreadful Chagas' disease, or even rabies. A number of people in Central and South America have died as a result of the vampire bite.

Most bats are harmless. They live on fruit and bugs. There is probably nothing to fear from the bat you may find in your attic. But we certainly don't want to be bitten by one, and especially by the vampire bat. People camping in Central and South America should be warned. A good warning can save a person's life.

Paul said that everywhere he went he warned people—not about bats but about evil and sin. They could do more damage than any bat. He invited everyone to find safety in Jesus Christ.

So everywhere we go we talk about Christ to all
who will listen, warning them and teaching them as
well as we know how.

Colossians 1:28 (TLB)

1. How do bats get around in the dark?
2. What do bats eat?
3. Why did Paul want to warn people?

THE SOONER WE COME TO JESUS CHRIST, THE LESS WE WILL BE HURT BY SIN.

NATURE'S CLOWNS

The otter doesn't take life too seriously. If it had its way, everything would be a game and a few laughs.

The otter's idea of a good afternoon is to get together with a bunch of friends. They will take turns sliding down a wet hill on their bellies. A few minutes later, otters might play Follow the Leader. If these games get boring, they can hardly wait to start a wrestling match with their brothers and sisters.

King James I of England enjoyed watching otters play. He kept a collection of otters and used them to catch fish.

The otter is an intelligent animal, and makes an excellent pet. As wild animals, they have a terrific bite; but when tamed, they can be good friends.

Sometimes they especially enjoy people. The sea otter has been known to swim alongside a boat and check it out. If the people are sleeping, the otter may climb on in. At the slightest noise, he takes off for the sea again.

Otters are fun-loving clowns, but they are more than that. When necessary, they are excellent hunters. Their favorite meals are bass, crab, crayfish, and sometimes an unsuspecting bird. Their hunting habits can be terribly messy. Too often an otter will take one bite out of a fish and then throw it away. When we find a few half-eaten fish, we can almost be sure an otter has been around.

Otters have beautiful fur. This is one of the reasons they are hunted in many areas of the world. It is also the reason why sea otters are afraid to come to land. Their slick fur coat does a great job of keeping them warm in cold waters.

They seem to prefer water, but otters can get along on land. In Europe, they make long trips from one lake, across the mountains, to another lake.

Like the fox, otters take time to train their young. Each one can hunt and swim before it leaves its parents. The mother may spend a full year before she releases her young. Otters often grow up to three feet in length.

The otter can take life seriously, but it also enjoys itself. Good times are a healthy part of their lives.

Sometimes Christians take life too seriously. If we aren't careful, we will forget how to laugh, play, and enjoy ourselves. Not everything should be quiet and dull. A good laugh or a funny game will help most of us stay healthy.

A cheerful heart does good like medicine, but a broken spirit makes one sick.

Proverbs 17:22 (TLB)

---

1. What do otters do for fun?
2. Why are otters hunted?
3. When was the last time you laughed out loud?

LAUGHTER CAN BE A GIFT FROM GOD.

9

THE RATTLESNAKE'S ENEMY

It doesn't scare easily. The short, chubby badger will take on almost any enemy. Even the poisonous rattlesnake isn't safe around this fighter.

Most of us would stay away from a rattlesnake. They are extremely fast and definitely deadly. But the badger, a three-foot-long rodent, thinks it is just a little quicker. After dancing around a snake, the badger will make a fast dash for the back of its head and the snake is finished.

Their odd appearance shouldn't fool us. Badgers are speedy. They can run almost as fast backward as they can forward. They can also dig faster than most machines. If a badger sees a human being or some other foe, the badger will start burrowing into the ground. In two minutes it will have enough of a hole to completely disappear.

Badgers' ability to dig helps them tremendously when searching for food. A badger will find a hole and smell a rat, mouse, or snake. In a second, it starts tearing the hole apart in search of its dinner. Once the badger begins, its victim often has little chance of escape.

Badgers enjoy the ground so much that badgers dig long, fancy homes. Their tunnels may stretch for thirty feet. Inside, they will have a special area just to hide from enemies. In another section, they will dig a nursery to place the five young they bear every year. Even when they catch food above ground, badgers still prefer to take it into their tunnel for meals.

Badgers have become a problem to some farmers because their natural food is becoming harder to find. They have now developed an appetite for farm animals, vegetables, and grain.

The badger has a strange relative and sometimes acts just like it. This cousin is the skunk. Mr. Badger can't give off the same odor as this stinker, but he does have a strong and noticeable odor of his own.

Anything that decides to fight a badger is in for a real battle. A badger can defeat a dog twice its size and give a grown man a terrific struggle. With all this strength, you might think they wouldn't have to be sneaky, but they are.

If a badger is afraid, it can pretend it is dead. Its body will stiffen, and it will stop breathing. A person can turn it over, thinking the badger is lifeless. Then, suddenly, the badger will strike and tear a piece of flesh with its long claws.

Many people are pretenders just like badgers. We act nicely in front of our parents. We try to give the right answers. But when we are away from them, we often act differently. We might get into trouble in school, or go places where we are told not to go. Then we come home, looking like little angels with sweet smiles. We act one way when, in fact, we are something entirely different. We are merely waiting badgers.

God is concerned about pretenders. In the long run they will hurt themselves. We need to be kind and thoughtful around our parents and away from them.

🦩 🐘 🐛

You try to look like saintly men, but underneath those pious robes of yours are hearts besmirched with every sort of hypocrisy and sin.

Matthew 23:28 (TLB)

1. How long a tunnel could a badger dig?
2. How long does it take a badger to dig a hole large enough to disappear into?
3. Why are people "sneaky" instead of honest?

HELP US TO DO WHAT IS RIGHT ALL OF THE TIME.

10

LOST AND CONFUSED

The lemming is a small field animal that is related to mice and rats. It enjoys the northlands and multiplies rapidly.

The amazing thing about these small animals is the trip that kills many of them.

Lemmings depend on grass, moss, and small plants to live. Though they are small rodents, they are big eaters. Scandinavian lemmings move in large circles as they eat everything in sight. Soon they are spreading in large numbers across highways, farms, and ditches.

Some lemmings go all the way to the sea looking for food. They soon leave the shore and start swimming. When they get tired, they can't turn around, so hundreds merely drown.

People used to think lemmings were killing themselves intentionally. There certainly was no way to get across the huge sea. Now we have a better answer. In their search for food, lemmings cross many rivers and lakes. They can be excellent swimmers. When they come to the sea, the lemmings probably think it is just another river, so they jump in. The lemmings swim until they are exhausted, then die at sea.

This doesn't happen every year to lemmings. Their numbers increase and decline. After several years of healthy growth, there are so many they have to keep moving. Only a small group of lemmings throw themselves into the sea.

They have a fancy name, but lemmings are really field mice. Some are fat, some are brown, and some are white. They are busy little creatures, constantly looking for food and having babies.

Like other small animals, the lemming has to be on the watch for enemies. None is a worse enemy of this little rascal than the snowy owl. When the lemming population is high, this owl also has more little ones. Owls move across the countryside, and their breeding depends on how many of these tiny mice are running around.

The lemming leads a short, busy, dangerous life. Those that reach the sea have finally become lost and confused. It looks like a river, but there is no way to swim it. Because they can't think it through, they perish.

Jesus Christ described us as something like this. Apart from God we would be lost. We wouldn't know good from bad. We wouldn't know about heaven, where we can live with God.

Christ invites us to believe in Him and become His followers. Each of us can be safe by becoming Christians.

For the Son of man came to seek
and to save what was lost.

Luke 19:10 (NIV)

---

1. Why do lemmings jump into the sea?
2. Where do they live?
3. Do you believe in Jesus Christ, the Son of God?

THANKS FOR BEING OUR GUIDE IN A CONFUSING WORLD.

11

WHERE DID THE BUFFALO GO?

Pretend you are riding a train across the plains of Kansas in 1870. You stick your head out the window and see large buffalo walking along the tracks. Then you look at the countryside, and as far as you see there are thousands of buffalo.

They aren't really buffalo. Their actual name is bison, but we have called them buffalo for hundreds of years.

When the white man arrived in America, the buffalo roamed from the eastern coast to the west. By 1819 they had been entirely killed off in the east.

The killing of the buffalo was especially hard on Native Americans. Many of them depended on the buffalo for life. They ate buffalo meat. They used hides for shirts, dresses, and shoes. Buffalo fur became blankets and robes. Tepees were made of buffalo hide. The hooves were boiled to make glue. Buffalo bones were carved into sleds, their horns were used for spoons, and muscles were made into bowstrings.

Native Americans didn't waste any part of the buffalo. They knew their survival depended on keeping these animals around. They were excellent hunters. One way of getting meat was to chase the buffalo toward a steep cliff. The buffalo would run over the edge and be killed by the fall. The Native Americans then had plenty of food and clothing for the winter.

Whites had little or no respect for the bison. They had rifles that made hunting easy. Rather than use the entire buffalo, they shot them for silly reasons. Some collected only buffalo tongues. They killed the animal to take a tongue worth twenty-five cents. They would hunt all day, kill one hundred buffalo, and make twenty-five dollars. Others took the hides at $1.25 each. Hunters destroyed thousands of buffalo, thinking they would always be there.

From 1865 to 1885, almost all the buffalo in North America were killed. That quickly, sixty million bison were destroyed.

The animal was almost entirely lost. Today they are being raised on ranches, and the number has grown greatly. But we came very close to destroying them.

God has been generous in supplying animals for humans. Some are for fun, while others are good workers. Many make excellent food. None of them are to be wasted.

Too many people want to kill merely to kill. Others will even torture animals. God is not pleased when humans are cruel. Animals are created to be used, but never wasted.

A good man is concerned for the welfare of his animals.

Proverbs 12:10 (TLB)

1. How many buffalo lived in North America at one time?
2. How much did bison tongue sell for?
3. Why did God create animals?

IT NEVER MAKES SENSE TO WASTE GOD'S GIFTS.

12

THE TARGET-SHOOTING FISH

It's really hard to believe. For years scientists laughed and said it couldn't be done. How can a fish spit water at a tree branch and hit a dry bug, which then falls into the water and becomes the fish's dinner?

Today we know the truth. Archerfish can shoot water as far as fifteen feet in search of a victim. They are highly accurate at hitting a ladybug six feet away.

Millions of us have never seen them because archerfish live off the coasts of Asia and northern Australia. They enjoy tropical waters. There might be other types of fish in these areas that have not been studied well.

Some archerfish spend most of their lives far out at sea. They are unable to use their special "gun." But the ones that do come to shore are excellent marksmen.

Archerfish are now kept in captivity in the United States. They are popular attractions. In some places, hamburger is sprinkled in fine pieces along the wall of the tank. The archerfish will shoot the meat off the side.

In order for a fish to do this, it has to overcome a couple of problems. One of these difficulties is sight. Since the archerfish stays in the water, how can it see clearly enough to aim straight? Somehow its eyes overcome the distortion.

The second problem is spitting with that much force. Somehow it traps water in its gills and with great power forces it through the mouth. Its tongue both pushes the water and forms a tunnel to help aim. In some ways it is much like a person spitting.

Archerfish may be especially intelligent. One reason for believing this is their ability to learn. Archerfish do not shoot insects from birth. Their aim is terrible, and they can't shoot far enough.

This is why they have to practice. If they stay at the job long enough, they develop strength and accuracy. Even as adults they are not always good shots. When an archerfish shoots too quickly and without good aim, it might miss its dinner by far.

Archerfish face the same problem as people. If we don't practice, we usually get sloppy and don't do well. Whether it is reading, baseball, or Ping-Pong, we do better if we stay at it.

A smart parent will help a child practice being good. Sometimes it doesn't come easily. But the more we choose to be kind, sharing, and careful, the easier it becomes.

Train up a child in the way he should go: and when
he is old, he will not depart from it.

Proverbs 22:6 (KJV)

---

1. **How far can archerfish shoot?**
2. **How does an archerfish learn to shoot?**
3. **Is it easier to practice being good or bad?**

THANKS FOR PARENTS WHO EXPECT US TO PRACTICE BEING GOOD.

13

ANIMALS THAT HIDE

Have you ever broken your mother's favorite dish? Right away you wished there were some place to hide. It would help if you could become the color of the wall and no one could see you.

If you were an animal, it might be easy to escape. Some creatures match the forest or desert so well you could practically step on them without knowing it.

The white-tailed jackrabbit does this extremely well. It lives in the cold north and mountainous areas. When the snows come, this rabbit turns white. It can flatten itself so even the sharpest eye will miss it. In the spring the same rabbit turns brown-gray and is just as difficult to find.

Coyotes blend into their background, and this makes them excellent hunters. They can sneak up on their dinner because the coyote is the same color as the field.

If we had to choose the animal that is the easiest to find, it might be the zebra. Some states used to dress prisoners in black-and-white stripes to make them easy to see. But don't be fooled. The zebra can be terribly hard to find.

The zebra lives in central Africa and likes to stay in crowds. Their herds may number twenty or sometimes grow to one thousand. If it had its way, the zebra would merely stay with its own kind and munch grass all day.

Sometimes they are captured and used as horses. The result is usually a disaster. They have mean tempers and can't be trusted. A zebra isn't afraid to kick and can do a tremendous amount of damage.

If not for man, the lion could be the zebra's only natural enemy. It would seem the zebra is an easy victim for the lion. Actually, zebras can put up a terrific fight. They have sharp teeth and can kick a lion dizzy. When three or four zebras start smashing a lion, it may wish to be home.

Usually, lions go hunting just before dark. This is when the zebra stripes start working. In the half-dark dusk of the evening, they are extremely difficult to see. What seems like a strange color combination really helps the zebra disappear.

Even in the gray evening, God would have no trouble seeing the zebra. No one can hide from Him or get lost in the crowd. Wherever we are and whatever we are doing, we are still under the careful eye of God.

Each of us is special to our heavenly Father. When no one else knows what we are doing, He does. He knows about the good things we do even when no one else thanks us.

If I try to hide in the darkness, the night becomes
light around me. For even darkness cannot hide
from God; to you the night shines as bright as day.
Darkness and light are both alike to you.
Psalm 139:11–12 (TLB)

1. How does the white-tailed jackrabbit hide?
2. How does a zebra fight a lion?
3. Who carefully watches us day and night?

GOD LOVES ME AND STAYS AROUND ME ALL THE TIME.

14

THE ZOO ON YOUR SKIN

If you want to see exciting wildlife, there is no need to head for the thick jungle. There are strange and crawling creatures living on your arms, legs, and face. A strong microscope would show us great surprises.

A few of these creepy monsters come from harmful fungus, such as athlete's foot or ringworm. The fungus is alive and growing like little mushrooms between our toes. Athlete's foot is a common problem.

Other living things on our bodies look like tiny bugs. They are called mites. Everyone has small, dry flakes of skin. The mites love it. They eat the skin flakes for regular meals.

No amount of baths will get rid of these small visitors. Warm water seems to make them grow and multiply. But don't be too concerned. Most of these microscopic creatures are good for us. One type of creature is often eating another kind. It is happening right now as you sit there. If they didn't eat each other, we would get too many of one kind and that wouldn't be healthy.

Dead skin falls off all day long. In twenty-four hours we probably drop ten thousand flakes. Most of the dust we see around the house is actually particles of dead skin.

Adults are continuously concerned with dandruff. Actually, there is no need to worry. Dandruff is not alive. It is harmless, dead skin.

44

While we are looking at our heads, we might as well check into the follicle mite. A follicle is the hole from which a hair grows. There are probably 120,000 of them on your head. Each is like a small factory, and its full-time job is to manufacture hair.

The follicle mite loves making a home in these tiny holes. A lazy creature, it merely rests and eats delicious bacteria. If it gets thirsty, a tall glass of hair oil will do the trick.

These mites sound unpleasant, but they really are friends. Most people have them. They actually help keep the head clean.

A few people are born without this little jungle on their body. Usually, they are in trouble. Their skin can't fight the bacteria that will attack them.

Sometimes we think everything important has to be big. We need all these little things on our bodies and we can't even see them. Little people are very important. A little bit of kindness goes a long way. Just a little "thank you" can brighten someone's day. God loves the little things we do because we belong to Him.

"Fine!" the king exclaimed. "You are a good man.
You have been faithful with the little
I entrusted to you."
Luke 19:17 (TLB)

1. What is a follicle mite?
2. What is usually dropping from our skin?
3. How many little things can you name that God uses?

THE IMPORTANT THINGS IN LIFE AREN'T MEASURED BY THEIR SIZE.

15

THE ANIMAL IN ARMOR

Animals find the most interesting ways to protect themselves. One kind of lizard can change colors, skunks send odors, and porcupines stick little spears in their enemy. None of these ways is more amazing than that of the armadillo.

This chubby creature is able to grow a real armored suit on its back. In some ways it is just like the old suits worn by knights hundreds of years ago. When the armadillo is finished growing, it looks something like a tank.

A special overcoat spreads across its back, neck, and sides. It is made of bones. A small piece of skin is between each round bone to hold them together.

If someone attacks an armadillo, it could do several things. It could try to run away. It might turn around and fight with sharp claws. If neither of these works, the armadillo will wrap up into a ball with the armor blanket to protect it.

The armor suit will hold off most enemies. But it is no match for an angry jaguar, which will smash the armor.

Armadillos have a real enemy in people. Their flesh is considered excellent eating by many. Others use the armor for baskets. After the animal has been removed, the shell is carried upside down like a purse.

Some armadillos are found in the southern United States. They are found more often in Central and South America.

Not only do they make good tanks, but they can become fairly tough battleships. When they come to a large creek, they are able to inhale great amounts of air. Their body parts fill up like small balloons. Then the armadillo crawls into the water and starts to swim.

In some areas the number of armadillos is going down. The number seems to be growing in Louisiana, Florida, and Mississippi. They are hunted often, but they do not disappear. Armadillos would come farther north, but they can't stand frost.

An average armadillo dinner would be a handful of maggots, ants, or termites. On special days, they eat fresh snake.

The armadillo found in the United States is called the nine-banded armadillo. They almost always have four young born at one time. New babies begin to develop their stonelike shell at once.

In some ways we are like the armadillo. We need protection against the evil and sin around us. It is easy to give in and do things that are wrong. After all, everybody else disobeys, steals, and lies.

God says there is a way to keep from doing these things. We need to depend on God and follow Him. When we do, He wraps His arms around us and gives protection.

So use every piece of God's armor to resist the enemy whenever [Satan] attacks, and when it is all over, you will still be standing up.

Ephesians 6:13 (TLB)

1. What is the armadillo's armor made of?
2. How do armadillos cross large creeks?
3. Name one way God protects us from sin.

GOD WRAPS US IN ARMOR TO KEEP US SAFE.

16

WHICH IS THE "RIGHT" WHALE?

The captain brought the boat to a stop and cut off the engines. Rocking quietly on the water, we watched and listened for any sign that whales might be close at hand. My wife, Pat, and I had traveled many miles to Nova Scotia, Canada, in search of this magnificent sight.

Suddenly, a huge body rose to the water's surface. We had trouble containing our excitement. This tremendous forty-five-foot long, fifty-ton creature had risen from the deep and parked itself close by.

The sea monster we met was called a right whale. Reportedly, whale hunters of old gave them this name because it was the "right" whale for hunting. This particular mammal was fairly easy to catch, produced a great deal of oil, and seldom sank after being harpooned.

Our watery friend remained visible for ten to fifteen minutes. Dependent on breathing air, it surfaces to fill its lungs and then dives deep into the Bay of Fundy. Right whales look like they are wearing hats but actually have white skin patches on their heads.

Suddenly, we saw the creature begin to move and arch its back, preparing to dive. And then it did. Going headfirst, the whale tossed its gigantic tail straight up into the air on its way down.

Their tails are called flukes. It's an awesome experience to watch them hoist straight up and then slide into the massive sea.

We remained in the area for two or three hours while the whale parade came and went. We possibly saw as many as twenty whales that afternoon. Many shot water eight feet high out of the hole on top of the head.

We understand the right whales never get a toothache. That's because they have no teeth. Some whales do have teeth and enjoy fish or squid for dinner. But the right whales are baleen whales. Not exactly picky eaters, they do strain their food and munch mainly on the smaller stuff.

There are "right" whales and "wrong" whales, depending on what you are looking for. For many reasons this was the "right" whale for whale hunters because it supplied their needs. If they kept chasing the "wrong" whales, they might not have earned enough money to support their families.

Smart people learn early that life is filled with right and wrong decisions. If we make the right choices, we can live at peace with God. The wrong choices could leave us sad and disappointed.

The Bible encourages us to go after the right choices.

Learn to do right! Seek justice, encourage the oppressed. Defend the cause of the fatherless, plead the case of the widow.

Isaiah 1:17 (NIV)

1. Describe the right whale's hat.

2. Why don't they get toothaches?

3. How can we learn what is the right thing to do?

HELP ME KNOW THE DIFFERENCE BETWEEN RIGHT AND WRONG.

17
BUGS WITH FLASHLIGHTS

We used to catch them in glass jars. When we had a half dozen or more it looked like a lantern. The light given off by fireflies in the jar was enough to read by. In the late spring and summer they filled our backyards. When we held them against our finger, we felt a little heat each time they flashed.

At the time the flashes didn't mean anything to us. But each one meant a great deal to the flies. (Actually, they are beetles.) They are sending out messages to flies of the opposite sex. The male might go forward and hold his light on for half a second. The female waits two seconds, then sends back a flash. If the flashes are not timed correctly, the fireflies stay away.

Sometimes a firefly will get its signals mixed up. It might hold a flash too long or wait too long to send it. The result may send it to the wrong insect. Because its signals were off, it could then be eaten by a stranger. It is possible that some types send out the wrong signals on purpose. They aren't looking for a girlfriend—just dinner.

Many of us call the firefly a glowworm. The entire subject is easy to confuse, since there are two thousand different types of bugs with lanterns on their tails. Often both names are used for the same insect.

The firefly can control its light. A substance that can burn fills the firefly's tail section. When air gets to this section it starts a small fire. The

51

firefly can hold the substance back or push it forward. That is why fireflies are sometimes hard to catch. They simply turn off their lights. The air is breathed in so the firefly can stop the signal whenever it wants to.

In the winter fireflies become coal miners. They dig into the top of the soil to escape the cold. If we were to dig them up, we might find their lamps still lit. They could be getting heat from their lanterns.

Fireflies are used for beauty and light. In other countries some women wear them on their dresses or jewelry. Men who have had to travel in the dark often make lanterns from them or put them on their boots to light their paths. The fireflies will become excited and light more often.

In some ways you are like a firefly. Jesus Christ told us to let our light shine before men. When people see our good behavior and the kind things we do, we are like a light shining in darkness. When they see this light, they can then see the God we serve. Like fireflies, we control our light. We can make it shine as much as we want to.

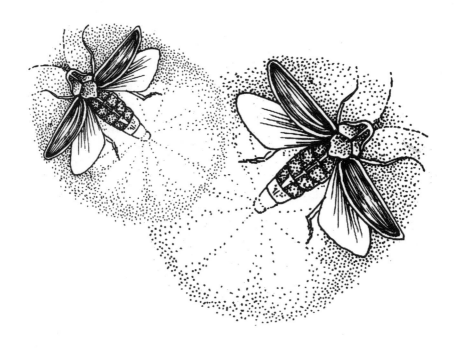

In the same way, let your light shine before men,
that they may see your good deeds and
praise your Father in heaven.
Matthew 5:16 (NIV)

1. What is another name for the firefly?
2. How many types of bugs have lanterns on their tails?
3. What are some ways you let your light shine?

A DARK WORLD NEEDS MORE LIGHT.

18

BIRD BUFFET

There is a popular eating place about twenty miles from where I live in Nebraska. The food is so good at this dining area that five hundred thousand (half a million) sandhill cranes stop there every year to sample the salad bar. And they enjoy it enough to tell their friends and come back again each March.

Cranes travel from their winter homes in Texas and Mexico. Their flight will take them to their summer homes in far-off Alaska and Siberia.

Plenty of birds migrate, flying great distances between seasons. But this trip is definitely different. During this journey the half million birds squeeze into a small area like the middle of an hourglass. If it's easier, picture a belt pulled very tight on a tiny waistline. These cranes come from many areas to land at this same restaurant.

What's so great about this bird buffet on the plains? Mostly it's the food. Cranes enjoy the corn special left sprinkled over the farmers' fields. Corn adds a bit of fat to a crane's diet to help this feathery friend along its way.

But no self-respecting crane likes to leave without snacking on the other treats. They may munch an earthworm here or slurp an insect there. Dessert might be a slimy snail or a piece of small plant.

Not only are the meals delicious but also plentiful. Thousands of the cranes stay around for three or four weeks, happily trying to put on weight.

With so many visiting birds, one would think the fields would be packed with temporary nests. But don't worry, there is more than enough motel space. Cranes sleep standing up in the shallow riverbed of the Platte River. They seem to feel safe there in case some animals try to attack them.

Cranes are fortunate. They can't farm, but there is usually plenty of food. They can't cook. It's hard to imagine a crane wearing an apron, putting burgers on a barbecue. Not every field is as nutritious as these few square miles in Nebraska, but birds normally do well.

If God treats cranes like they are valuable, think how much more valuable people are. That's why we help feed other people. They are valuable to God, too.

God provides for us, and we help God provide for others. That's one way we see how good our heavenly Father is.

Look at the birds of the air; they do not sow or reap or store away in barns, and yet your heavenly Father feeds them.

Matthew 6:26 (NIV)

1. Where do the cranes spend their summers?
2. What do cranes eat at this bird buffet?
3. What is one way we can help God feed other people?

HELP US TO BECOME THANKFUL FOR THE WAY GOD MEETS OUR NEEDS.

19

THE MIGHTY GORILLA

The tall man couldn't believe his eyes. He had come a long way from Europe to study the gorilla, but he didn't expect this. There in the branches of a tree was a bed. It was made by tying the limbs together, and the tying was finished with real knots. Gorillas are intelligent enough to tie a double-over-and-under-twist knot. The largest ape in the world is an amazing animal to study.

We may want to study gorillas, but they don't want to study us. This huge African creature would rather be left alone. He is a quiet banana eater who isn't looking for an argument or fight with anyone.

Gorillas live in the thick forests, whether in the mountains or the lowlands. Those living in the higher regions grow thicker coats to fight the cold. Some people think gorillas are nearly as intelligent as people. Others who work with them deny this. One thing is for sure—if you get a chance

to fight a gorilla, DON'T! With one swing of its powerful arm, a gorilla can tear your entire shoulder off. If it grabs your leg, it can rip the whole limb away.

Gorillas are family animals. They have the cutest, quietest little babies. Their families often travel together. In some areas they are members

of large groups. Nigeria has an entire nation of gorillas living together.

We often see pictures of gorillas walking on their two legs. Many of them do. But they can also move on all four limbs. Older gorillas rely almost entirely on all fours.

It would be hard to guess just how strong gorillas really are. They probably don't fully realize it, either. We do know a gorilla can bend a piece of two-inch tempered steel. Beyond that, it is hard to tell.

A gorilla has a strong body but is still weak. It is weak because it can't think well enough to stay out of trouble. Gorillas will charge at men carrying rifles and get themselves killed.

Strong people are often weak in the same way. We don't stop to think. Later we are sorry because we did something stupid.

The Bible can be a big help. It holds excellent advice. We can learn how to avoid trouble. We can get strong guidance from God. The fool says, "I don't need advice." The really strong people are the ones who look to God for direction.

A wise man is mightier than a strong man.
Wisdom is mightier than strength.
Proverbs 24:5 (TLB)

1. What can a gorilla bend?
2. Do gorillas travel alone?
3. How can the Ten Commandments keep us out of trouble?

THANKS FOR MAKING US STRONG BY GIVING US DIRECTION.

20

CRYBABY CROCODILES

When someone cries hard, we say that person is shedding crocodile tears. The saying is not so silly, because these long creatures are big criers. They aren't pushing big tears because they are sad. Their bodies can't handle all the salt they get, so they cry to keep their bodies clean.

Don't let the tears fool you. Crocodiles aren't softhearted. They will eat anything, from a tiny beetle to a baby hippopotamus. If they fail to find one of these, another crocodile or a human will do just as well.

These long, funny-looking creatures can get their prey two ways. Their powerful tails can take a victim down in a second, and their crushing jowls can finish it off. Their speed demands a great deal of respect. Only man or another crocodile attacks one.

Crocodiles move so smoothly and quietly that they can pluck a bird off the water. They can be excellent fishermen. One crocodile was opened up in South Africa, and twenty-two sets of dog licenses were found inside.

Crocodiles' green color and lumpy skin make them hard to be seen. They merely lie still and look like a log or clump of weeds.

The crocodile's nearest relative is the alligator. For most of us, the two would be difficult to tell apart, especially if they were chasing us. The easiest difference can be seen in the mouth. When a crocodile closes its mouth, some of its teeth stick out. Alligator teeth all fit inside.

After a crocodile attacks, it will drag its victim to a hideaway and let the dinner rot. This is probably because of the crocodile's teeth. They are excellent for attacking but poor for chewing. They don't line up straight.

Crocodiles carry rocks in their stomachs. They even gobble down soft drink cans and bracelets. Scientists think the rocks help digest food.

At one time the Nile River in Egypt was crowded with crocodiles. Today they are gone, all except for an occasional lost one that may wander in.

Some pharaohs of Egypt became proud and thought they were special. They didn't think they needed God or anything He had to say.

God sent the king a message. He told him not to be so proud. Next to God he was nothing. The pharaoh saw himself as a mighty lion. God looked at him as simply a crocodile blowing bubbles in the river.

Often we get too proud of ourselves. We think we are the smartest, the fastest, the trickiest. Why do we need God? Look at all we can do. God tells every bragger to calm down. You are just blowing bubbles in the river. If you really have good sense, trust and follow our living God.

Son of dust, mourn for Pharaoh, king of Egypt,
and say to him: "You think of yourself as a strong
young lion among the nations, but you are merely
a crocodile along the banks of the Nile, making
bubbles and muddying the stream.
Ezekiel 32:2 (TLB)

1. How do you tell an alligator from a crocodile?
2. What color are crocodiles?
3. To what did God compare a proud king?

TEACH US TO DO GOOD BUT NOT TO TALK ABOUT IT.

21

THE BAD-TEMPERED RHINO

One of the loneliest creatures in all the outdoors is the grumpy rhinoceros. Not only is it short of friends, but even its enemies stay away.

Rhinos have a great deal going against them. Part of their problem is their lack of intelligence. Frankly, they do some dumb things. Another source of trouble is their nearsightedness. They don't see well and therefore don't trust anything or anyone.

For instance, most animals know when people are around, and they get out of the way. Not the rhino. It doesn't know humans are close until they get next to it. Frightened, the rhino will suddenly attack rather than hide. Pity the poor jeep or truck parked nearby. The rhino will ram it into a junk heap.

The female rhino even has trouble getting along with boyfriends. If the female sees a male she likes, she backs up and charges him. She knocks him down and steps on him just to say she likes the boy. Kindness doesn't come easily to her.

In spite of its size, the rhino isn't slow. It can turn quickly and gain a speed of thirty miles an hour. Not bad for two to four tons.

The rhino begins as a bulky baby. The kangaroo is only the size of a quarter at birth, but the rhinoceros weighs sixty pounds on the first day.

Humans have hunted the rhino until there are few left. Today only thousands of these African "tanks" exist. There are laws to protect the rhino, but they are often broken. They are sometimes killed just for their horns. There is a story in Asia that says, "Anyone drinking from a rhino horn cannot be poisoned." Those who believe this pay a large amount to buy the useless cup.

Others think dried rhino blood is good medicine.

There are few happy moments in the life of a rhino. They don't seem to get along with anything, including other rhinos.

The brightest spot in a rhino's life is a little tick bird. These birds land on the huge monster's back and help out by eating the ticks and other dangerous insects off the rhino's skin.

If the rhino takes a nap (often standing up), the tick bird will be a watch bird. Should danger come, the bird picks itself up and starts screaming. The rhino wakes up immediately, ready for whatever is coming.

All rhinos know is how to attack and fight. On more than one occasion, they have charged full speed into moving trains. With all of this bad temper, a little bird has become the rhino's only friend.

Our neighborhoods, schools, and churches have people who are lonely. They need a good friend who will spend time with them. Someone who won't tease them or treat them badly. They are lonely for a friend just like you.

I have called you friends.
John 15:15b (NIV)

---

1. **How does a female rhino treat a male rhino?**

2. **Why are rhinos hunted?**

3. **Name one person you think might need a friend.**

SOMEBODY NEEDS MY FRIENDSHIP.

22

Birds That Swim

This is one way of describing the penguin. They seem to have wings but can't fly. Their beaks and eyes look like they belong to a creature in the sky. Scientists insist it is a member of the bird family. So far the penguin isn't convinced. It merely waddles along on the ice and swims in the cold sea.

These aren't the only things that make the penguin different. If it can't be a bird, it has at least decided to be a helicopter. It might swim to the side of an ice bank, then shoot straight up out of the water. Penguins' wings flap like propellers. They can do it with such force that they land feetfirst on the ice.

A penguin looks funny when it walks. Its heavy body and short legs give it a comical look.

Despite their clumsy appearance, penguins aren't so easy to catch. Not that their enemies don't try. A sea bird, the skua, enjoys penguin eggs and baby chicks. But skuas can't fight a healthy penguin. They steal eggs if the adults don't watch carefully. If the nest is guarded well, the skua birds act as a team. One will distract the penguin while the other carries off an egg.

Adult penguins are usually safe from the leopard seal. These enemies swim in the sea and wait for penguins. Most healthy, careful penguins can avoid their tough hunters.

Penguins build their nests in areas called rookeries. Thousands of

them get together but keep their homes a safe distance from each other. They love to be with a crowd. These neat-looking creatures chatter constantly.

They aren't afraid to fight. The close distance between their nests invites plenty of arguments. An angry penguin will peck its opponent and hit with its flippers.

Generally, penguins don't grow tall. A foot and a half is probably average for the Adélie variety.

When they build their nests, the mother and father play different parts. Dad is in charge of finding materials, while Mom takes care of construction. One by one, Dad collects pebbles from the shoreline. Work isn't their favorite sport, so if a nest is left unguarded, a neighbor will probably steal a couple of pebbles.

God has sprinkled His earth with fascinating characters and sights. They are each a reminder of the imagination and wonder of our Creator. It is amazing what God can do.

He quiets the raging oceans and all the world's clamor. In the farthest corners of the earth the glorious acts of God shall startle everyone. The dawn and sunset shout for joy!

Psalm 65:7–8 (TLB)

1. Why are penguins called birds?
2. When are they "helicopters"?
3. Can you see God's work in nature? How?

WITH GOD'S IMAGINATION, HE DIDN'T SETTLE FOR A DULL WORLD.

23

THE TWELVE-INCH TONGUE

A friend offered me a delicious-looking piece of chocolate candy. Naturally, I ate it without asking any questions. When it was safely in my stomach, my pal broke up laughing. He had given me a chocolate-covered ant.

Ants aren't part of my diet if I can help it. But the giant anteater and its relatives love them. They spend most of their waking hours looking for a delicious meal of live ants.

It would be hard to call the anteater cute. The largest one in Central America can grow to eight feet in length. It has a long nose, though not all anteaters do. The tongue is often one foot long so it can lick up as many ants as possible.

The anteater appears to be tiptoeing. It walks on its knuckles instead of flat-footedly. It may be trying to protect its claws, but that's just a guess.

Under the best conditions, this creature isn't fast. When it has a baby anteater, it moves even slower. For the first year of baby's life, the mother carries the infant on her back. She must be terribly tired at the end of the day.

Not all anteaters roam the fields. Some, such as the three-toed anteater, live in trees. Its diet is made up of termites and insects moving in the branches.

Anteaters look lazy and friendly, but don't be fooled. The silky anteater can be mean. It likes to sleep in a tree branch during the day. If a strong wind blows, it simply sleeps on. But let a person or animal shake a branch, and Silky wakes up with a violent temper and takes a swing with its claws straight out.

Most anteaters prefer to travel through life alone. When two are seen together, they are most often mother and child.

Anteaters have their share of persistent enemies. The small anteaters are hunted by eagles, hawks, and owls. The larger ones are attacked by jaguars and other large cats. In a battle between the two, an anteater will hold its own with its long, sharp claws.

These claws also come in handy when looking for food. An anteater will open a decayed log, smashing it with its claws. The bewildered ants try to run in any direction to get away. This is when the remarkable tongue comes to work.

Not only is the tongue extremely long, but it also has a sticky glue. The anteater's saliva is like flypaper, and ants are gobbled up by the scores.

The anteater needs its long tongue to get into cracks and corners. It licks out each valuable piece of food.

Tongues are fast and helpful to both animals and humans. They are not only important for eating but also in controlling our talking.

The psalm writer was glad he had a tongue. It gave him a chance to praise God. In song, testimony, and teaching, our tongues explain how we feel about our heavenly Father.

My lips shall greatly rejoice when I sing unto thee;
and my soul, which thou hast redeemed. My tongue
also shall talk of thy righteousness
all the day long.
Psalm 71:23-24 (KJV)

1. Why do anteaters walk strangely?
2. What hunts anteaters?
3. Name two ways our tongues can praise God.

THE WISE PERSON'S TONGUE SPEAKS WELL OF GOD.

24

Pearl Divers

Instead of becoming a lawyer, policeman, or doctor, have you ever considered a job as a pearl diver? If you enjoy swimming and exciting work, this may be just what you need. You may have to move, since the best pearl diving is done on the Persian Gulf. Usually, two men go out together. One stays in the small boat while the other dives for pearls. By merely holding his breath, the diver drops one hundred feet to the bottom of the Gulf. For one minute, he fills a basket full of shells and then takes off for the top. The man in the boat pulls the basket up with a rope. This is terribly dangerous. The only reason these men can do it is that they have grown up practicing it a few feet at a time. Normally, we think of pearls as white or pink. But actually, they come in a large selection of colors. Some are bronze, brown, green, or possibly blue. One of the most expensive pearls is black.

Pearls are the only valuable gem presently taken from living creatures.

Most of the pearls we think of come from oysters. But they can grow in a number of shellfish of the mollusk family.

Pearls begin when a tiny speck of sand or other material gets inside the shell. The oyster is bothered by it in the same way that dust hurts our eyes.

The oyster starts to cover the piece of sand so it won't be painful. Layer after layer of covering finally turns the speck into a pearl. Some of the pearls end up lovely and round, while others are odd shaped.

Most of the pearls we see are plastic. They aren't worth much but are fun to wear and play with.

Not all the great pearls are found in Persia. One highly valued pearl was discovered near Paterson, New Jersey, about 140 years ago. It weighed 1.64 ounces, or 45.92 grams.

But maybe diving isn't for us. Don't let that stop you. There are plenty of people catching gorgeous pearls who never dive. They have opened pearl farms.

The job still isn't easy. The "farmer" keeps a large bed of shells. He places a tiny piece of sand in each shell. Twice a year the owner cleans each one of seaweed and sticks. After seven years it's ready to open. One out of twenty shells holds a usable pearl.

People have loved pearls long before the birth of Christ. Job knew how valuable they were during his lifetime. One day Job was thinking about all the foolish things people do. They pick bad friends and get into trouble. Sometimes they do the exact opposite of what their parents tell them. A few break the law.

Job thought how much better it would be if people took time to think of the right things to do. Doing what is good would be more valuable than the black pearls of the Persian Gulf.

The price of wisdom is above pearls.

Job 28:18 (RSV)

---

1. Describe how divers collect pearls.
2. How are pearls farmed?
3. Give two reasons why people get into trouble.

THANKS FOR SHOWING US WHAT IS IMPORTANT IN LIFE.

25

MONKEYS IN A HOT TUB

Often it is hard to change the way we live and act, but we can do it. That's what animals find out. They change when they really have to.

Some of the macaque (pronounced *ma-KACK*) monkeys in the mountains of Japan discovered that they could change when they really wanted to. This type of monkey prefers the warmth of India or Malaysia, and normally when it gets cold in northern Japan, they head for the lower regions. That was true until one day a few of the monkeys decided to make a change.

They looked over the hot tub (or volcanic springs) high in the freezing mountains. Soon they began to enjoy those warm swims and thought this felt pretty comfortable.

Despite the snow that covered the rocks all around them, the macaques liked hanging out and taking baths. Even when the snow stuck to their heads, they could simply duck beneath the surface and wash it off.

Some of the monkeys changed their behavior and spent the winter in the cold. Other monkeys thought it was a terrible idea and headed down to a milder climate. They decided to come back in the spring.

This kind of change in nature isn't as unusual as it might sound. A few types of birds that may have flown at one time don't fly anymore, like the ostrich or the penguin. Rhinoceroses used to live in Nebraska, but that doesn't work anymore. Elephants roamed the middle of America at one time, but they are all gone. Jaguars living in Central America might be moving farther north toward the United States.

Nature does not always stay the same. Animals give up old habits and start new ones. Change is sometimes an excellent idea whether we are talking about macaque monkeys in Japan or young people who go to school.

Human beings often do bad things. We might be rude or even lie or cheat. Too many of us have stolen something or been terribly unkind to another person. Most of us have done some really nasty things.

The good news is that we can change. We may not be able to change everything about us, but we could begin to obey better, become kinder, and not take anything that doesn't belong to us.

Monkeys can change the way they behave, and so can human beings.

Keep your tongue from evil and your lips from speaking lies. Turn from evil and do good; seek peace and pursue it.

Psalm 34:13–14 (NIV)

1. Where do macaque monkeys enjoy a "hot tub"?

2. Which birds probably used to fly and don't fly anymore?

3. Is there something you should change in your life?

HELP US GET RID OF THE BAD HABITS WE NEED TO GET RID OF.

26

THE BIG EATER

The next time you carry the groceries in from the car, be thankful. If you owned an elephant, you would need to bring in half a ton of food every day. On top of that, the elephant would drink a small tank of water.

Elephants aren't very practical pets, but they are fascinating animals. They are the largest beasts to walk on earth.

Besides their size, elephants are best known for their two large teeth, called tusks. Both males and females have them. Elephants have been hunted just to collect their tusks. They are called ivory and have been used for their beauty. Each tusk can weigh up to three hundred pounds.

Elephants have a better set of teeth, which stay hidden in their mouths. These teeth crush the fruit, grass, or leaves that elephants' trunks pull up for lunch.

The trunk is one of the handiest tools of any animal. It may look odd, but it does a long list of jobs. The trunk works as a fork, shovel, and picker. All day long it collects food and pushes it into the huge mouth. It also doubles as a hose. The trunk isn't really a straw. An elephant doesn't drink through it. It fills the trunk with water and then squirts the water into its mouth.

If the elephant gets an itch, the trunk becomes a back scratcher. When the elephant's owner wants a ride, the trunk turns into an elevator. On a hot day, trunks make great showers. The African elephant has a trunk shaped like two fingers at the end of it.

Elephants prefer to live in the wild, but in India they have been trained. Sometimes they are used to plow farms. Others are used as freight trucks to carry heavy loads. Wealthy people ride elephants to go tiger hunting. During war, elephants are put to work as tanks to smash through the enemy.

Human babies take nine months to develop before they are born. Elephants need twenty-two months. They live a long time, and some are probably sixty years old.

In areas where elephants roam free, the farmers aren't too happy to see them. They often move in herds of ten to one hundred. If they become hungry and move onto a farm, they could eat the place bare in a few hours.

The stories about elephant burial grounds are not entirely true. They do not appear to all go to one central place to die. But not everything is known about elephants' death practices.

Elephants are animals of habit. They may move for hundreds of miles, and each year they follow the same trail. Some countries have built highways on old elephant paths.

Elephants do the same thing over and over again, but the stories of their good memories are untrue. Elephants appear to forget as easily as any other animal.

When it comes to forgetting, human beings are especially good at it. We forget our lunch money, our homework, and even our phone number. If we were elephants, some days we might forget about our trunk.

One thing that we should keep repeating to ourselves is how kind God has been to us. It would be easy to forget His goodness and just think about what we *don't* have. God gave us better memories than elephants so that we could remember our Creator.

Bless the Lord, O my soul, and forget not all his benefits.

Psalm 103:2 (KJV)

---

1. How much does an elephant eat?
2. How do elephants drink water?
3. Name three good things God has given you.

WE COMPLAIN OFTEN WHEN WE FORGET HOW GOOD GOD HAS BEEN TO US.

27

Nature in the City

While it's fun to hike mountain trails or spend the afternoon in the forest, they aren't the only places we can enjoy nature. Many of us who grew up in the city enjoyed watching the wildlife that lived among the buildings.

One of the most interesting of the downtown birds is the beautiful pigeon. Their relatives like to live among the rocks and are often called rock doves. But many animals, just like people, have moved to towns and cities.

Pigeons build nests on high ledges, where they lay eggs and raise their families. The baby pigeon is born blind but soon gains its sight after being fed carefully with pigeon milk. In about ten weeks, the young bird is able to fly around the neighborhood all by itself.

Pigeons prefer some form of grain, but they are not picky eaters. Often, they are happy to hop and walk around a city park and eat the food humans share with them. Living with people has allowed them to feel comfortable with children, and sometimes they get close if the child is quiet and gentle.

Not everyone likes to have pigeons living on their block. One of the biggest problems is that pigeons go to the bathroom wherever they want. Benches, sidewalks, cars, and strollers might get rock dove droppings on them.

Some people eat pigeons. In parts of China a pigeon's heart was considered very special and was eaten by some wealthy men.

Other people like to raise pigeons. They might keep rock doves in a cage or on their roof or in the backyard. Homing pigeons can be taken hundreds of miles from home, and they will return to their owners by using special skills that we don't fully understand.

When Jesus Christ was a little over six months old, His parents, Joseph and Mary, went to Jerusalem to dedicate the baby to God. Obeying the Old Testament practice, they brought two pigeons along. These were a sacrifice to give to the Lord.

As he grew up, Jesus probably saw many pigeons where He lived and might have enjoyed feeding them. When we see a pigeon, we could remember how important it is for every child to belong to God and grow up to love Him.

And to offer a sacrifice in keeping with what is said in the Law of the Lord: "a pair of doves or two young pigeons."

Luke 2:24 (NIV)

1. What is a rock dove?
2. Where do pigeons live in the city?
3. Why do parents dedicate their babies to God?

EVERYONE COULD DEDICATE THEIR LIVES TO GOD.

28

Can Dolphins Talk?

Jill Baker will never forget the amazing rides she used to take. When she was only thirteen, a dolphin started visiting the beach near her home in New Zealand. People would come for miles to see the unusual creature.

Normally, untamed dolphins stay away from humans. But this one was special. Almost every day he would swim close to shore and entertain the people. Those who watched named him Opo.

At first the dolphin was cautious. Opo would let people pet him. As time went on, he became more playful. Opo started to play ball with the crowds. Sometimes he would balance a bottle on his nose.

The year 1956 was an exciting one for everyone who got to see Opo. But it was a very special time for young Jill. The dolphin developed an extra fondness for this teenager. If Opo was playing with others when Jill came, he left them immediately. He would dash to her side like a pup for its dinner.

Sometimes Opo would come up behind the young girl and pick her up. He would then take her for short rides around the beach.

Soon a law was passed that made it a crime to harm any dolphin in Hokianga Harbor. The people wanted to protect Opo, their new friend with the large black fin across his back.

This is a true story. Though Opo has since died, the people who visited the beach remember him well.

Some of this isn't too hard to imagine. After all, a dolphin is one of nature's smartest creatures. Most of the famous porpoise shows are really starring dolphins.

Usually, dolphins travel as families. The parents and children swim side by side. When one is injured, its family will come to its aid. They will push their kin to the top of the water so it can breathe. If possible, they will keep it up until the dolphin can swim for itself.

Dolphins are smart enough to have their own way of talking—though they can't say words. They can make clicking sounds, whistles, or even barks. Their dolphin friends can understand the sounds and answer in the same way.

Some scientists believe that we will someday "talk" to dolphins and listen to them. By understanding their clicking sounds, we might be able to know what they are saying.

We can talk because we have vocal cords in our throats. Not dolphins. They make sounds by blowing through the nose, whistling, or even smacking their mouths. The sound travels well through water, and a dolphin's child can hear it far away.

Being able to talk is a good gift from God. It's too bad some people use it to hurt others. Life would be hard if we couldn't say anything. We need to use our voices to say things that are kind and caring. Even the dolphins care about one another.

Therefore each of you must put off falsehood and
speak truthfully to his neighbor, for we are all
members of one body.
Ephesians 4:25 (NIV)

1. What was unusual about Opo?
2. How do dolphins "talk"?
3. How should we use our voices?

HELP ME WATCH THE WORDS I USE.
SHOW ME HOW TO MAKE SOMEONE
FEEL BETTER BY WHAT I SAY.

29

CANNIBAL INSECTS

The praying mantis is one of the big eaters in nature. It will even eat other praying mantises.

This bad habit often begins at birth. The first insects to hatch may start eating the other mantis eggs. From then on they would just as soon eat another mantis as anything. If one happens to land near its brother, it just might be eaten.

Even the ones that seem to like each other don't really like each other. After the male and female get together to mate, the female will then eat the male. The male seems to realize this and accept it. He could fly away. But he seems to know it is now his time to become her supper.

After she has finished the meal, the mother mantis will lay her eggs. These eggs are stuck together in cases. She might lay several cases at one setting.

This big appetite isn't all bad. Mantises are a great help to farmers and gardeners. Every day they eat insects that otherwise would destroy crops.

They don't care what they eat. Plant lice, spiders, butterflies, wasps, grasshoppers, flies, bees, and caterpillars are all part of their diet. In some cases, they have even attacked moths, hummingbirds, and garter snakes.

The mantis is tame to human beings. We can hold them and never be bitten.

One of the reasons mantises are such successful hunters is their color.

They are green and look just like a blade of grass. They can sit motionless for hours.

During most days the insect will eat enough food to equal its own weight. This would be like a young person eating seventy-five pounds of food daily. They take their time and pick out every edible part of their prey. When the mantis is finished, it will lick its hands much like a kitten does.

There are over fifteen hundred types of mantises. The praying mantis folds its hands, but its victims aren't sure it is religious.

The mantis is such a successful eater that farmers will even buy them. Some dealers will sell cases of eggs. As they hatch, the young mantises begin to feed on the pests that destroy crops.

Eating this much is good for the praying mantis. Their bodies can handle all this food. But eating all the time is bad for humans. Our bodies can't take it and soon may become sick.

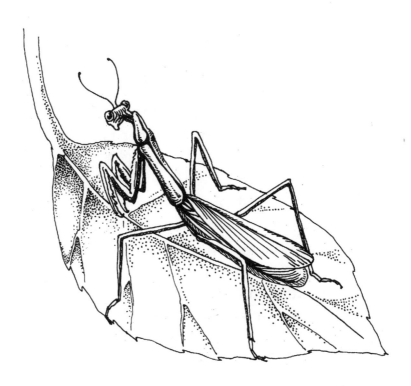

God cares enough for us to even discuss our eating. In the Bible, He tells us to eat no more than we really need. He wants us to be healthy.

The good man eats to live, while the evil man lives
to eat.

Proverbs 13:25 (TLB)

1. How many types of mantises are there?
2. What color is the mantis?
3. Why does God care how much we eat?

THANKS FOR A HEALTHY BODY.

30

A Lazy Creature

Isn't it terrible when someone calls us lazy? Most of us aren't, really. There are things we don't like to do, but other times we can move quickly.

What hurts is to get the nickname "lazy." We don't deserve it, but the hairy sloth does. It moves only when it has to.

If a sloth is left alone, it will sleep for eighteen hours a day. It can sleep upside down holding on to a branch. Sloths aren't intelligent animals and don't care to get much done. It takes them an entire minute to move just fourteen feet.

My wife and I were fortunate to see a sloth in the rain forests of Costa Rica. As expected, the creature was hardly moving at all, but we did detect an arm in slow motion reaching for a branch.

The sloth lives in Central and South America. There are two types. One has two toes on each foot, and the other has three. They look somewhat the same, but their bones and eating habits are different.

A sloth spends most of its life hanging upside down. Its hair grows away from its stomach instead of toward it.

As the sloth sits almost motionlessly in the hot jungle, tiny plants grow on its fur. This is called *algae*. It looks like green moss and gives good protection to the sloth. Sloths often look like they are part of the trees. Some people confuse them for a termite nest hanging from a branch.

Sloths are too lazy to be friendly. Most of the time they don't want anything to do with other sloths. Usually, if two are seen together, they are a mother and child.

The closest sloths get to being active is when they happen to get into the water. They are excellent and fearless swimmers.

Fortunately, they don't have to catch their food. They probably would never get around to it. Almost their entire diet consists of leaves from the Cecropia tree.

There aren't many enemies for the sloth to fight off. When they are young, eagles try to catch them, but otherwise they are left alone. Sloths might be too lazy to defend themselves.

Laziness is all right for some animals, but it is a terrible habit for people. God knows lazy people are in for a long road of trouble. The person who does her work immediately and does it well will be a happy individual. The person who puts everything off is asking for hard times.

A lazy fellow has trouble all through life;
the good man's path is easy.

Proverbs 15:19 (TLB)

1. **Where do sloths live?**
2. **How long do sloths sleep?**
3. **What do we call a person who puts off doing her work?**

THANKS FOR WARNING US AGAINST BECOMING LAZY.

31

UNDERGROUND FOUNTAINS

If you ever get to Yellowstone National Park, you can see water explode out of the ground. The water jumps 120 feet into the air. The place is called Old Faithful. Almost every hour its beautiful shower leaps up.

The earth holds a great amount of water. It gets there from melting snow and mountain streams. But some of the water can't stay there because it gets too hot. Just like a teakettle, it has to blow off steam.

It is no small job to jump out of the ground. Normally, the water in our pan at home boils when it reaches 212 degrees. Underground it has to reach 291 degrees before boiling. If the water will leap 120 feet into the air, it has to be much hotter. The earth must be extremely hot to cause a geyser to blow up.

As we are learning more about underground hot water, we are now beginning to use it. The town of Reykjavik, Iceland, sits on top of hot water springs. The people there now know how to heat their homes and run their industry by using the water boiling under their town.

The largest geyser to ever blow was in Waimangu, New Zealand. One day the steamy water broke through the surface and rose fifteen hundred feet into the air. This new geyser had enough force to lift a one-hundred-pound boulder far into the sky.

Some of the hot groundwaters contain valuable minerals. People often travel to these areas to help fight illness such as the gout or rheumatism. Hot Springs, Arkansas; Mount Clemens, Michigan; and Saratoga Springs, New York, are just a few of the areas that have health resorts built on hot water springs.

Despite the intense heat, some forms of life manage to survive inside geysers. In some areas algae have been found alive.

For thousands of years we have known there was water flowing under the ground. In some places we can drink the water that is running out the side of a mountain.

When the psalm writer saw things like this, his mind turned to the One who had made them. Water under the ground merely reminded him of how God supplied everything. He knew it all came from a loving Father.

Praise him who planted the water within the earth,
for his lovingkindness continues forever.

Psalm 136:6 (TLB)

1. What causes geysers?
2. How does Iceland use its underground water?
3. Why did groundwater remind the psalmist of God?

THE EARTH IS FILLED WITH SIGNS OF THE GOODNESS OF GOD.

32

THE TALLEST ANIMAL

If you could only teach a giraffe to dribble a basketball! From its front hoof to the top of its small horns, a giraffe can grow up to eighteen feet tall. This makes it the tallest animal in the world.

There are some myths about giraffes that still go around. Most of us have heard that the giraffe makes no sound. This is false. A mother giraffe calls her babies with a whistling noise. Giraffes can also make a strange gurgling sound. The next time you go to a zoo, listen carefully.

Another myth many believe is that giraffes are weak and defenseless. But anyone who gets into a fight with a giraffe soon finds out how wrong that idea is. A giraffe can use its head like a powerful club. When it fights another giraffe, both of them often end up with painful head wounds.

Even lions are careful around this tall creature. If a giraffe gives a good kick, it could kill the big cat.

When given a choice, giraffes would rather depend on their vision and speed. They have an excellent tower to see what is around them. Giraffes run over thirty miles an hour and give many enemies a fast race.

Giraffes have two ways of walking. When they aren't in a hurry, they merely pace. Their left legs move together, then both right ones. When danger comes, they take off in a gallop like a horse. First their front legs move, then their rear legs.

Baby giraffes have no choice but to be tall. They are born almost six feet high and weigh over one hundred pounds.

Their long necks usually help them, but sometimes they get in the way. The neck gives them good food selection. Giraffes eat leaves from the tops of acacia trees. When they want to eat leaves near the ground, they are in trouble. Their necks will not reach that far. They have to spread their legs and become "shorter." Only then can they come close to the earth.

A giraffe's neck is amazing for its size. Yet in some ways it is like any other mammal. It has seven vertebrae in the neck, like other animals. The only difference is that the bones are larger.

Each human being also has a fascinating neck. It is short but can turn quickly to either side so we can see what is going on.

When we are mad or upset, we do an interesting thing. Many of us sit still and hold our necks tight. We seem to be saying, "Nobody is going to get me to change." We have become stiff-necked, or stubborn.

This practice is dangerous. If our parents correct us, we shouldn't stiffen our necks and refuse to change. Sometimes we are wrong, and the smart person learns to admit it. God can't help people who won't change.

A man who remains stiff-necked after many rebukes will suddenly be destroyed—without remedy.

Proverbs 29:1 (KJV)

---

1. How many vertebrae do giraffes have in their necks?
2. How fast can giraffes run?
3. Name one way you would like to improve yourself.

GOD WANTS TO KEEP CHANGING ME.

33

NEAT BABOONS

If you visit a farm in Africa, you might get a huge surprise. In some places you will see baboons out in the fields picking fruit. They aren't stealing it. These large monkeys are so intelligent they can be taught to do simple jobs. They have stacked wood, herded sheep, and driven tractors.

The baboon is an exciting animal. Often four feet tall, they prefer to live on the ground, but some travel in trees. They might weigh 150 pounds. Baboons are quick animals that move on all fours.

The male baboon is larger than the female, who is usually more shy and eats less. Because of the differences, the male protects the female. Like human children, the female baboon grows up faster than the male. The male passes her in size later.

There are many stories of human children being raised by baboons. Most of them are merely made up. But at least one seems to be true. In 1903 a boy was captured with a troop of baboons in South Africa. He was named Lucas.

Lucas had developed the characteristics of a baboon. He showed his teeth, barked, and ran on all fours. After a year in the hospital, he got a simple job. Lucas never learned to talk and died in a few years.

Not everyone thinks baboons are cute. They have terrible reputations for raiding farms. In large numbers, they will steal crops and other food.

Baboons are able to plan their attacks. Farmers believe they send out scouts to inspect an area before raiding it. If the scouts see men with weapons, they go back and tell the others. They also appear to place scouts to watch while the others sleep.

A great part of the baboon's day is spent looking for food. They eat vegetables and search for them for twelve to fourteen hours a day.

Many people consider the baboon ugly and dirty. The truth is they are among the cleanest of animals. Part of the reason is their love of grooming.

If you want to make a baboon happy, merely spend an hour combing its hair and picking ticks. This is the way baboons treat each other. Most baboons spend several hours a day grooming and being groomed.

Baboons seem to use it to impress one another. They take pride in their neatness. After an argument they make up by grooming each other. If a male and female like each other, they may pick each other's ticks. The baboon being groomed often rests on its back like a kitten having its tummy rubbed.

We all live longer because we stay clean. Those who don't, often have germs and become sick. But washing the body can only do so much. We also need to have our minds cleansed.

People of all ages think about doing unkind things. We may think about hurting someone, or stealing or telling a lie. God will help us by cleaning our minds. Jesus Christ promised to help those who follow Him.

Now ye are clean through the word which I have
spoken unto you.

John 15:3 (KJV)

---

1. How "intelligent" are baboons?
2. Why do they like grooming?
3. What can I do when I think about hurting someone?

HELP ME KEEP MY MIND CLEAN.

34

ROBINS ARE GOOD PARENTS

The beautiful red-breasted robin is one of the most-loved birds in the United States and Canada. They visit lawns and backyards all over the country.

Robins are probably most famous for their ability to pull worms out of the ground. They do a slick job of it. No other creature does it quite as well.

These friendly birds aren't limited to worm dinners. They also enjoy a fresh caterpillar, a wiggly spider, or a poky snail. Robins can destroy some fruit, like cherries, but their help far outweighs the damage they may do.

Robins are strictly fair-weather fowl. When the autumn winds turn cool, robins head south. The spring daylight will call them to travel thousands of miles again to their homes.

The best place to see robins moving north is along the Mississippi River. They fly low over homes and farms. They push hard each day, as some have to get all the way to Alaska.

When a robin returns to my neighborhood, it is looking for my house on 9th Street. The father robin can remember the area he left six or seven months ago. He arrives before the mother so he can reclaim his old grounds. Some fighting may go on as new birds try to find a nesting place. Soon it is all solved and the females come home.

During this time the male sings loudly. His song says this is his land and others should stay away. Father robin is getting ready to raise his family.

When the mother robin arrives, she has a busy job ahead. She needs to build a strong nest to hold her eggs and new chicks. The male will help collect materials, but the female will gather most of them.

The nest is built like a bowl. It is usually a three-stage operation. The outer part is made of sticks and twigs. An inner lining is made of mud. If no mud can be found, the mother will take dry earth in her beak and dunk it in water. The final step is a soft cushion of tender grass.

She is a good mother, looking out for her young.

Two or three times she will lay eggs in this nest. It may take twenty hours for a baby robin to break open its shell. The mother sits tight. There are some things a chick must do for itself.

Both mother and father get busy feeding the helpless newcomers. They have to collect food quickly to avoid cats that love to catch robins.

Often storms will throw baby robins from their nests. Usually, the best way to help them is to leave them alone. They are difficult to feed, but the mother robin will try to find them and bring them food.

Robins are "only" birds, but they work hard at being excellent parents. Sometimes we forget how much our parents work for us. They not only earn money, but they also provide our food and clothing. We like to complain, but most of us have terrific parents.

Children, obey your parents in the Lord, for this is right. "Honor your father and mother"—which is the first commandment with a promise—"that it may go well with you and that you may enjoy long life on the earth."

Ephesians 6:1–2 (NIV)

1. How does a male robin select a home?
2. What is the mother's job?
3. Give three reasons why you are glad for your parents.

THOSE WHO HAVE GOOD PARENTS ARE WEALTHY AND SOMETIMES DON'T REALIZE IT.

35

HOW DUMB ARE DONKEYS?

If you would like a donkey for a pet, don't worry about not having a ranch. There is one type of donkey that grows only thirty inches tall. It never gets as tall as a yardstick and can be fun to keep.

Donkeys are strong, tough-skinned animals that used to do a large share of people's work. Today there aren't as many, but they still have strong backs.

Donkeys usually stand three to five feet at the shoulders and like to keep to themselves. People aren't their favorite friends, so they stay away if they can. Even during hot, dry seasons, when donkeys become terribly thirsty, they still will avoid humans.

The donkey is something of a family creature. Its family, called a *troop*, isn't like ours. Usually, a troop consists of a father (called a stallion), several mothers, and a handful of youngsters. A troop will consist of ten to twelve donkeys.

The stallion takes his job seriously. He is the great protector of the troop. The father makes sure everyone in his "family" is safe from harm.

Generally speaking, the donkey has only two enemies. The first one is humankind. People hunt donkeys, and their number has gone down greatly. The donkey's second problem is the wolf. Donkeys have nothing to fear if they stay together. But if one wanders off or gets lost, a wolf could catch it.

If most donkeys had their way, they would stay in the hot, dry land. They might enjoy the mountains but still prefer them to be dry.

Often we know about the mule better than the donkey. They aren't the same, but they are relatives.

A mule is an odd animal. It is the product of a father donkey and a mother horse. The result is a tough, strong, and somewhat intelligent animal.

Mules can carry from two hundred to three hundred pounds. They get along better in hot weather and are less likely to overeat or drink. Mules aren't picky eaters and can gulp down almost anything. They will also put up with more from a careless owner.

In many areas mules have been more valuable than horses. George Washington thought mules were just the animal a young nation needed.

The biggest problem with a mule is that it can't have baby mules. There is only one way to have a mule: There must be a donkey parent and a horse parent. Mules cannot reproduce themselves.

In the southwestern United States and Mexico, there is a small donkey called the burro. Many of them live in the wild and roam the deserts.

Some people look at donkeys as pickup trucks. They are small and stocky and can carry heavy loads for long distances.

But dumb? That's another matter. In some ways they are smarter than people.

The prophet Isaiah put it clearly. He said the donkey knows who its master is. People aren't always as intelligent. Often we forget about our God and Creator. We begin to go our own way and ignore God. In this case, who is really dumb—the donkey or the person?

The ox knoweth his owner, and the ass his master's
crib; but Israel doth not know,
my people doth not consider.

Isaiah 1:3 (KJV)

---

1. What is a mule?
2. What is a stallion?
3. How are donkeys sometimes smarter than people?

THANKS FOR REMINDING US THAT WE HAVE A MASTER IN HEAVEN.

36

THE BAD-NAME LION

When the early pioneers crossed America, they found large numbers of lions. They weren't the huge cats from Africa, but they were their relatives.

The cougar, or mountain lion, was one of the most famous cats they found. It was an animal with a strange scream, which put fear into anyone who heard it.

Over the centuries, cougars have probably lived all across the nation. They like rocky areas with plenty of places to hide. Normally, they are happy hunting small game. Often, their dinner consists of just a bird.

When small animals are hard to find, cougars attack deer and sometimes farm stock. They have killed sheep, cattle, and horses. Usually, they drag a large victim to another spot and cover the body. The animal is eaten for several days.

In spite of its rough reputation, the cougar is a thoughtful mother. She might give birth to five cubs every year. She guards them carefully. For the first seven months, she feeds them on her own milk. When they get older, she brings them bones and meat.

It will often be two years before she lets them loose.

The cougar played a large part in the life of some Native American tribes. Apaches had great respect for the frightening scream of the mountain lion. They believed this sound meant someone was going to die. They used cougar paws to chase away evil spirits. Pictures of cougars were painted on the walls of caves in hopes of getting kind treatment.

White men did not have the same regard for the cougar. They hunted cougars and shot, poisoned, and trapped them. Today, few cougars exist, and most of them live in hard-to-reach sections of the country.

Cougars are dwindling in numbers because they have a bad reputation. Some of the stories about them are true. They have killed farm animals and may have killed a child or two somewhere in history. There are also a large number of false stories told about them. Most of us cannot separate the truth from the folklore. Cougars have such bad names that people continue to kill them even if they aren't sure why.

The same thing happens to children and young people. They get into trouble at school or in the neighborhood. Soon they have a bad name. People don't know if they can trust them. Later they get blamed for things they didn't do. But that is easy to happen once you get a bad reputation.

Few things in life are as important as a good name. It has to be earned by good behavior.

*A good reputation is more valuable than
the most expensive perfume.*

Ecclesiastes 7:1 (TLB)

---

1. How long does a cougar stay with its mother?
2. How long does a mother feed her young her own milk?
3. Describe someone you know who has a "good" name.

I WANT TO LIVE IN SUCH A WAY THAT I CAN BE TRUSTED.

37

THE BUG THAT EATS WOOD

We can only guess how much damage a termite does. Every day these busy little insects are eating wood from homes, sheds, barns, garages, and offices. They do hundreds of thousands of dollars worth of destruction every day in the United States.

A man in Seattle was sitting in his kitchen, leaning on the table. Suddenly, it collapsed, throwing him to one side. Termites had eaten their way through the floor and ruined one of the table legs.

Termites will attack some living trees, but most of them enjoy a good snack on dead wood. A few prefer it wet, but most want it crunchy-dry.

This is a strange insect, because it eats something that isn't healthy for it. There is something in wood called *cellulose*. A termite's stomach can't digest it. But there is a tiny creature, so small it can be seen only with a microscope, that lives in the termite. This one-celled organism eats the cellulose so the termite can get nourishment from it. Otherwise the termite would be eating wood and getting sick.

Termites are excellent at finding wood. It is possible that they can even smell it. Some types can dig under the ground and travel over one hundred feet. When they decide to come up, it will be directly under a tree.

One species of termite starts out in a quiet way. A female and male will dig into a piece of wood. They then make a glue and close up the hole. The queen starts immediately to lay eggs. Their family starts to grow and the children begin to eat the wood. Sometimes the family increases slowly. By the time the owner discovers the termites, his furniture will be practically wrecked by the little creatures.

The oddest termites live in Australia. The queen termite lays as many as three million eggs every year. She may live for twenty-five years. In her lifetime, this termite queen could lay seventy-five million eggs. To do this, her body has to swell to gigantic size.

The biggest enemy to the termite is the ant. Termites are usually afraid of this pesty relative. Some termites fight off ants with a sticky glue that comes out of the top of their heads. Ants get stuck in it and are left helpless.

When termites get inside a piece of wood, it may look solid. But it is being destroyed without our knowing it. The Bible says a person who is proud is also hurting himself and doesn't know it.

Most of us like to brag. We say we are the best, the fastest, the smartest. But someday we are going to get hurt. People will stop being our friends. Someone will outrun us or get a better grade. It is good to be honest about our ability. We get hurt by bragging.

Pride ends in destruction; humility ends in honor.

Proverbs 18:12 (TLB)

1. How do termites eat cellulose?

2. How many eggs can a queen termite lay?

3. How can we lose our friends?

KEEP US FROM BRAGGING.

38

THE HUGE SUN

The sun doesn't look too large hanging in the sky. If I put a quarter up to my eye, the entire sun is blotted out. This is merely the way it looks. The sun is so big that it is difficult for us to comprehend it.

We know how large the earth is. It is so big we will never visit most of it. There are a few parts that haven't even been studied well.

The earth would be just a small speck against the sun. The sun is so large that the earth could be placed in it over 1,250,000 times.

This tells only part of the story. The sun is a star, and not even a big one! It is medium sized. Half of the stars around it are even bigger. Space is enormous, and we have only begun to study it. The sun is only one of the one hundred billion stars in the Milky Way.

The sun is a great help to the earth. It supplies heat and light. The sun is so powerful that in one second it can give off all the energy humans have used from the beginning of time. In one second!

We get most of our light from the gas surrounding the sun. It is about two hundred miles deep.

The sun is so hot that we couldn't even begin to get close to it. If a small dot were as hot as the middle of the sun, the heat from the dot would be strong enough to kill a horse standing one hundred miles from it. Naturally, this is impossible, but the illustration shows us the tremendous heat of the sun.

We are in no danger from the sun, because it hangs ninety-three million miles away from us. In early July it is actually ninety-four million miles away.

There is some concern that the sun will burn out. If it does, the people on earth could be in serious trouble. But this isn't the type of problem that should keep you awake tonight. If the sun does burn out, it will take at least five billion years to turn to ashes.

One of the most colorful sights in nature is to watch a beautiful evening sunset. If you can see it in the country, it looks like melted butter and syrup. That sunset should be a good reminder to us. If you are angry about something, get rid of it before the sun goes down.

Sometimes we can't help getting upset. A person may have cheated us or told a lie. But don't carry around a chip on your shoulder. If you stay angry, it might begin to make you a mean person. Drop your anger before the sun goes down.

If you are angry, don't sin by nursing your grudge. Don't let the sun go down with you still angry— get over it quickly.

Ephesians 4:26 (TLB)

1. How long would it take the sun to turn to ashes?
2. How much bigger is the sun than the earth?
3. What should we do with anger?

HELP US CONTROL OUR ANGER BEFORE IT HURTS US.

39

SNAKE STORIES

Has anyone ever told a story about you that wasn't true? That really hurt, didn't it? Sometimes the stories pass around and soon people think you actually did it.

For hundreds of years snakes have suffered from the same problem. They don't know it, but false stories are often spread about them.

Some of the stories we hear about snakes are true. They can be poisonous, but nine out of ten snakes are harmless. A few people who have been bitten by poisonous snakes have died in less than one minute, but most people live.

It is true that some snakes can swallow a victim larger than its mouth. An Asia python can gulp down an entire small deer.

Snakes can be amazing climbers. Black snakes can race through the top part of bushes as fast as they can move on the ground. Often snakes are excellent tree climbers.

Do snakes lay eggs or give birth to their young alive? Both are true. Most of them hatch from eggs. About one-fourth are born straight from the mother.

Most false stories probably started because we are afraid of snakes. Because of fear, it is easy to stretch the truth and imagine things that we didn't see.

Someone started a rumor about the coral king snake. It is often called the "milk" snake. The name started when a person reportedly saw a king snake climb a cow's leg and milk the creature. There is no truth to this, but people still tell it as fact.

Mud snakes have long had an odd story told about them. They sleep in a neat circle that looks like a wheel. For years people have claimed the mud snake can put its tail in its mouth and chase people like a hoop or wheel.

Another rumor got started about the mud snake. Some claim it has a poisonous sting in its tail. This is far from the truth. If it is frightened, a mud snake might shake its tail in a menacing way, but it's only bluffing. The tail can do no more damage than a string.

But these are only the beginning of myths about misunderstood reptiles. Snake charmers do not really control snakes by music. Snakes are deaf and merely follow the movement of the charmer's head.

If we kill a snake, its mate will *not* hunt us. A snake's tongue is harmless. If a snake is seriously wounded, it does not always wait until sundown to die. Most snakes will not attack a human if they can avoid it. A snake is just as afraid of us as most of us are of it.

Life is filled with rumors and half-truths. Often, we aren't sure just what to believe. False stories hurt snakes, and some snakes are killed unnecessarily. Lies hurt people. Many lose friends and jobs because false stories are spread around. Jesus Christ had lies told about Him when He was on earth.

Before we talk about anyone, we should ask two questions: Is it true? Is it kind?

Lie not one to another.

Colossians 3:9 (KJV)

---

1. How did the "milk" snake get its name?
2. Name some false stories about snakes.
3. What two questions should we ask ourselves before we talk about anyone?

HELP US TO SAY GOOD THINGS ABOUT PEOPLE.

40

APARTMENTS IN THE FOREST

A rain forest isn't exactly an apartment house, but in many ways it seems like one. Filled with hundreds of monkeys, lizards, birds, jaguars, butterflies, sloths, snakes, and other creatures, it is packed with living species.

My wife, Pat, and I visited a rain forest in Costa Rica and were happily surprised. We were afraid it was one of those places where animals lived but we wouldn't get to see any. Not only did we see a large assortment of wildlife, but we heard their noises quite clearly.

We heard monkeys chattering at the top of their voices. There were birds singing and calling out to friends. We didn't hear the snakes, but we knew they were there.

One of our best sightings was the Jesus lizard. This little green monster gets its name because it looks like it walks on water. We saw it run rapidly, up on its hind legs, across the surface of the river. The lizard's light weight, flat feet, and excellent speed allow it to stay on top of the water for a short period of time. This was one of the most amazing and funniest animals we saw on our trip.

But back to the apartment house idea. Certain creatures live on the ground floor of the rain forest and seldom go very high into the trees. Other animals roam around in the middle section without going up or

111

down much. Still others have their living spaces in the tops of the trees. A few members of the top group might spend their entire lives up in the roof area.

A rain forest apartment house has all kinds of characters living there. Love birds coo away their time talking softly to each other. Butterflies dress beautifully as they flutter around. Howler monkeys talk loud and might keep some creatures awake. Earthworms crawl around on the ground eating leaves and the like.

Of all the "apartment" dwellers, the Jesus lizard is one of the easiest to remember. Every once in a while I remember that Jesus really did walk on a lake. Not because He had flat feet or because He ran across the water. His disciples saw Him walking on the surface, and He didn't sink.

Jesus Christ is the Son of God and can do all kinds of miracles. If nature has a funny lizard and its actions remind me of how great Christ is, I'm glad I haven't forgotten.

During the fourth watch of the night Jesus went out to them, walking on the lake. When the disciples saw him walking on the lake, they were terrified. "It's a ghost," they said, and cried out in fear.

Matthew 14:25–26 (NIV)

1. Name one place you can find a rain forest.

2. How is a rain forest like an apartment house?

3. How was Jesus able to walk on water?

THE SON OF GOD IS GREATER THAN NATURE.

41

THE MASKED BANDIT

Be sure to lock your doors tonight. If you don't, you could get a visit from a sneaky raccoon. These small animals can work a doorknob, and once inside they take what they want.

A raccoon's hands are small and easy to move. It can open your refrigerator and take out the honey. Don't be too surprised if the raccoon robs the cookie jar and dunks sweets in milk. Raccoons aren't choosy; they will eat almost anything. If they are thirsty, they will turn on your faucet.

Expanding cities don't seem to bother the animal with the black mask. Some have been found in downtown New York. Raccoons cross bridges at night to raid garbage cans.

Raccoons' ability to change has kept their numbers high. They would rather live in the forest but can get along in most places. Farmers aren't too happy with them because they steal corn and chickens.

If a raccoon could be given a test, it probably wouldn't prove very intelligent. But the raccoon is so clever that it can get away with almost anything. Some raccoons make beautiful pets.

When there is no danger close by, raccoons love to play. They are natural clowns trying to make life a game. It is almost as if they are trying to see how much they can get away with. Yet they have a healthy respect for their parents. When a baby raccoon gets out of line, the mother gives it a strong smack.

It would be a mistake to think of raccoons as just show-offs. They have

a nasty bite and are terrific fighters. The masked bandit can beat a dog twice its size. If a raccoon traps a dog near water, it is strong enough to drown its attacker.

Raccoons' favorite foods are often found in water. They rest by a stream and drag for crayfish and minnows. They are excellent swimmers.

With this type of personality, you can imagine how much raccoons enjoy a campsite. They will sneak in at night and steal practically any food left out. In the morning only open buckets and paper wrappers remain.

Raccoons can also be tender and loving. As with most animals, the mother takes good care of her young, which are called *kits*. If a mother raccoon dies, another mother will adopt the children.

Many people think of the raccoon as a favorite pet. Some even think it should be our national pet and its picture should be on our coins. The biggest problem with this cuddly creature is its constant stealing. It has no respect for the property of others.

In this way the raccoon is like too many people. It is easy to pick up things lying around. We think no one is going to miss it. We know it isn't ours, but we take it anyway.

Stealing is always wrong. We know how we feel when someone takes our things. God wants us to protect each other's property.

He who has been stealing must steal no longer.
Ephesians 4:28 (NIV)

---

1. What will a raccoon do in a house?
2. How do they treat orphan raccoons?
3. Have you ever had something stolen from you? How did you feel?

IT IS WRONG TO TAKE
WHAT IS NOT MINE.

42

GETTING AWAY FROM WINTER

When the cold snows begin to blow, many animals have to find a place to hide. Their bodies aren't made to live in the deep freeze. They also run short of food. When the leaves and grass are buried under ice, hunting becomes hard.

To get away, some animals will go to sleep. Bears, opossums, and skunks decide to take a nap. On a nice, warm day they might get up and go for a walk. This isn't hibernating, but merely taking a long sleep.

Other animals go into a deep sleep and their bodies change. This is called hibernating. Woodchucks, ground squirrels, some bats, and rodents are among those that hibernate. An animal's heart may beat three hundred times every minute when it is busy looking for food or building a home. In hibernation, its heartbeat drops to about four per minute.

The woodchuck is a good example. When it hibernates, its heart beats only once every five minutes. Most people would think it is dead.

Hibernation is a part of nature we know little about. Some animals begin their sleep in nice weather, during October or September. At least one animal actually pulls its shades down in July.

Children who want to investigate hibernation will want to visit bat caves. These are usually cool places. The hibernating bat hangs upside down and its body temperature drops. It is only a degree or two above freezing. But don't handle one or let too much light into the room. Bats that are disturbed can wake up and take off.

Some hibernators seem to get carried away. Certain ground squirrels drop off in midsummer and sack out for nine or ten months.

A few types of woodchucks get their hibernation backward. If the summer gets hot, the yellow marmot decides to find a comfortable bed. This is called *aestivation* and allows the animal to beat the heat.

Sooner or later all of us go into a deep sleep. It is something like hibernation, but we call it death.

When the Bible tries to explain death, it compares it to a heavy sleep. We close our eyes in death and open them to see Jesus Christ. It is much like going to sleep in your mother's bed and waking up in your own.

Like hibernation, there is much we don't know about dying. But we do know that death for the Christian means going to be with Jesus Christ.

For if we believe that Jesus died and rose again,
even so them also which sleep in Jesus will God
bring with him.
1 Thessalonians 4:14 (KJV)

1. **Do bears hibernate?**
2. **How slowly may an animal's heart beat per minute in hibernation?**
3. **What are the hardest and the best parts about death?**

CHRIST HAS MADE DEATH A VICTORY FOR THE CHRISTIAN.

43
THE BIGGEST CAT

The next time you are playing with a kitten in your backyard, remember this: This cat has relatives that are fourteen feet long and weigh over five hundred pounds. Don't worry about them coming for a visit, though, since most tigers live in Asia.

Tigers would rather stay away from people. Their meetings have usually been sad for both man and animal. Over the years, tigers have killed thousands of people. Work on the Chinese Eastern Railway had to be stopped because tigers were killing too many workers.

Humans haven't been too kind to this beautiful cat. Tigers have been hunted for their furs and blood. Some believe tiger blood is a helpful medicine. Others have killed this cat simply out of fear.

Though it is a big animal, the tiger is as quiet as a cotton ball. When looking for food, it can move through thick brush without a sound. Tigers are looking for practically anything—from giant elephants to river fish.

Their hunt for food is no small order. A tiger needs fifteen pounds of meat every day. If one attacks a large animal, it could eat fifty pounds at one sitting. Tigers will stay by a fallen deer and eat for several days.

It is a shame that people and tigers have not gotten along. The tiger has a lovely fur. Some have a rich orange color with dark black stripes crossing its body. Others are a light color coming close to white.

Tigers give birth to two to four babies at a time. These young ones stay at their mother's side for about a year. Tigers prefer to live alone but aren't

unfriendly. When two meet, they might stop, lightly rub cheeks, then move on.

The life of a tiger isn't easy. Even with its size, speed, and hunting ability, food is still hard to catch. The other animals get used to tigers and their ways; sometimes tigers go a week without catching any food.

Because of its huge body, the tiger has to search for food most of the time. It hunts at night and hides by a water hole during the day. If a tiger decided to stop looking altogether, it would soon starve.

The Son of God is important to each of us. We need to know more about His life, death, and resurrection. He told us we can know Him better by searching the Bible. It's the best way to find out more about our friend and Savior, Jesus Christ.

You search the scriptures, for you believe they give you eternal life. And the scriptures point to me!
John 5:39 (TLB)

1. Where do tigers live?
2. Why are their numbers going down?
3. Name three things you know about Jesus Christ.

WHEN WE LEARN MORE ABOUT CHRIST, WE LEARN MORE ABOUT GOD.

44

HIDDEN IN THE TREES

Hiking through a park, my companion quietly told me, "Look over there."

"Where?" I whispered.

"Under those trees."

Then suddenly I could see it. Three sets of beautiful dark eyes were staring back at me. Silently, three deer sat motionless, hidden in the trees. They did not rise to run. Nervously each looked back, wondering what we might do.

One of the things that nature does best is to hide. An animal could be resting in a tree and look little different than the branch it is sleeping on. A polar bear resting on the snow can barely be detected by the human eye.

Animals know that one of the safest things they can do is to not be seen. Zebras, for instance, can defend themselves, but they would far rather let their black-and-white stripes blend into the evening dusk. Other animals have trouble picking out a zebra just before dark.

Chameleons are excellent at hiding. They can control their color by blending into the color of the material around them. If a chameleon is on a green leaf, its body chemistry goes right to work. A mixture of yellow and blue in its body comes together to create a green color just like the leaf it is standing on.

These changes are made automatically and quickly. In a matter of seconds, the chameleon turns from yellow to brown. Sometimes the chameleon will change color for no other reason than it wants to meet a boy-friend. If it believes the occasion calls for dashing green, "Presto!" it takes on a different look.

People aren't so different. We can't change into purple people, but we do a little adjusting. If we are frightened, some of us turn pale or white. When we get caught doing something wrong or we are embarrassed, our faces could turn red or pink. Our lips could tremble or our eyes get wide when we are frightened. That's why we might hide our faces so no one will know how we feel.

Hiding our faces works better with people than it does with God. If we do something wrong or something good, God can see it inside our hearts. Putting our hands over our faces or pulling a blanket over our heads won't keep God from seeing the truth.

That's good. We can enjoy life much better if we don't try to hide our feelings from the God who loves us.

You know my folly, O God; my guilt is not hidden from you.

Psalm 69:5 (NIV)

---

1. How do zebras hide?

2. How long does a chameleon take to change color?

3. Why can we be glad that God sees our hearts?

THANK YOU FOR KNOWING WHO I REALLY AM.

45

THE EIGHT-ARMED SWIMMER

Did you ever try to shake hands with an octopus? If you did, you would have at least eight of them to shake. But stay away from the ones near the Antarctic. Some of them have forty arms.

There are many strange stories told about the funny-looking octopus, and most of them are true. For instance, there are large octopuses that measure thirty-two feet across the arms. They will stretch the length of most living rooms. Fortunately, they aren't often found. Twelve inches in diameter is the usual size.

Normally, the octopus doesn't care to fight. Hiding is its first choice. But when cornered, the octopus can put up a terrific fight. One type, living near Australia, has enough poison to kill a human being. Should a person get tangled in octopus arms, he or she could easily be drowned.

Part of an octopus's ability is to change colors. When one hides in seaweed, it looks just like the seaweed. In a minute it can become the same color as a rock. Even an old machine will be an excellent hiding place. One octopus can turn the same color as rust.

It has often been said that the octopus is a cannibal. That means it eats other octopuses. This is only half the story. Some will even eat themselves. One might start munching on its own arm—and eat another one for dessert. Octopuses don't usually do this unless they are old and near

123

death. But if given enough time, the arm will grow back. Even a wounded eye can mend itself.

A mother octopus has many babies. A female might lay fifty thousand eggs at one sitting. Few of these will ever become adults.

There are many sea creatures that enjoy octopus and octopus eggs. The laying of eggs marks the end of the female life. She dies soon afterward.

When in good health, the octopus can move quickly. It hurries backward through the water. It can suck water into its body and push the water out through a tube. The water leaving the body makes the octopus move backward rapidly.

One of the oddest features of the eight-armed monster is its ability to shoot ink. When in trouble, it gives off a dark liquid. This is all part of the octopus's disappearing act. The large cloud of ink hides the octopus while it finds a deep hole or underwater bush.

It would be fun if all of us could just disappear when we wanted to. We could shoot up a cloud and blot ourselves out. This would come in handy after we had broken a dish or come home late.

God has given us a better way. When we do something wrong and are sorry, He promises to blot it out. He won't remember it anymore. That is the kind of loving God He is.

Repent ye therefore, and be converted, that your
sins may be blotted out.
Acts 3:19 (KJV)

1. What does an octopus shoot out?
2. What are some colors an octopus can become?
3. What does God do with my sins?

THANKS FOR MAKING MY SINS DISAPPEAR.

46

FLYING SNAKES

You can relax. There probably are no snakes flying over your house right now. But don't say it absolutely definitely could not happen somewhere.

There is a snake that flies. It has no wings, and it actually does more gliding than flying. But it does leave a tree branch and sail through the air.

Moving quickly across a series of tree branches, the flying snake takes off in pursuit of its food. As it leaves the tree, the snake's body flattens out and goes into an S shape. By making its body wider, the snake is able to spread out like a kite and travel several feet through the air.

Landing on an unsuspecting victim, this skydiving reptile is soon eating a lizard burger.

Most of us have heard of flying fish. The butterfly fish of Africa can dart out of the water and glide for six feet before landing again. But what about the flying squirrel?

A flying squirrel has two parts that aid its ability to sail through space from tree to tree. First, its arms and legs stretch out like a cape. This allows the squirrel to remain airborne. Second, its large tail is used to control direction. Turn this way to make it go right. Turn the other way to go left.

These aren't the only airplanes to be found in the wild. I didn't see any flying frogs in Central America, but they tell me there are plenty. A few lizards may be able to do the same thing.

Amazingly, there are animals that we have not discovered. Maybe a few more flying or gliding creatures will be seen in the jungles, the sea, or the mountains.

Like birds, these unlikely animals have two reasons to fly. Either they are trying to catch their food, or they need to escape.

Each of us is going to be tempted to do some terrible things. We might want to lie or steal. Maybe we feel like cheating or starting a fight. Those are the times when we need to spread our arms and legs like a frog or a squirrel and get out of there.

We can't exactly fly, but there is a time to get moving. Escaping from a bad or dangerous situation can be the really smart thing to do.

Flee the evil desires of youth, and pursue righteousness, faith, love and peace, along with those who call on the Lord out of a pure heart.
2 Timothy 2:22 (NIV)

1. Name two animals that can fly.
2. How does this one type of snake fly?
3. Have you ever been in a bad situation and are glad you "flew" out of there?

DON'T BE TOO PROUD TO GET OUT OF THERE IF YOU NEED TO.

47

THE SEVEN-HUNDRED-POUND RACER

Be careful when walking on ice. Some of it is so thin that we can crash right through it. Yet a half-ton polar bear can run across the same ice and not even break it. Its speed and balance allow this white monster to do things humans can't match.

Not only are they light on their feet, but polar bears are fast. Normally, they don't chase people, but if they get hungry enough, no one is safe. They can sprint at twenty-five miles an hour and catch most men. Every once in a while, a human near the Arctic is killed by a polar bear.

Polar bears are good on ice and snow, but even better in the freezing water. A polar bear might hitch a ride on a floating iceberg or swim through the sea. Some of them enjoy the water so much that they spend most of their life afloat. Practically no animal is safe if this giant decides to attack. If it wants to, a polar bear will go after a boat and try to turn it over. That would be a frightening sight coming toward you.

The polar bear's favorite food is seal, which has little chance against the white ghost. It will lie flat on the ice and crawl close to its victim. The polar bear's color makes it difficult to see. Only its dark eyes, nose, and mouth can be seen. When the polar bear gets close enough, it makes a sudden lunge, and the seal is finished.

Part of the bears' quickness comes from the nonskid soles on their feet.

They have lived so long in the frozen Arctic that they no longer have snow blindness. Therefore, very little gets away from them.

Mother bear has her cubs venture out of the den in March. They wander in search of food. By summer, the cute little things will weigh over two hundred pounds and be ready to face life alone.

Papa bear isn't a big sleeper. The night is one of his favorite times for hunting food. He can pick up a scent and follow it for miles to find food.

Some polar bears are yellow or gray, but most of them are white, with beautiful fur.

If the polar bear were red or green, its life would change. Its victims would see it coming and most could get away.

The psalm writer was thinking about his own life and the things he had done wrong. His sins were like dark spots on his life. He asked God to forgive him and take the marks away. When God forgives our sins, we become whiter than the fresh snow—even whiter than a polar bear.

Sprinkle me with the cleansing blood and I shall be clean again. Wash me and I shall be whiter than snow.

Psalm 51:7 (TLB)

1. How fast can a polar bear run?
2. What is its favorite food?
3. What happens if we tell God about our sin and ask Him to forgive us?

THANKS FOR FORGIVING AND FORGETTING MY SINS.

48

THE VAMPIRE INSECT

It isn't easy to get away from mosquitoes. They live in every part of the world except the ice lands surrounding the North and South Poles. They live almost everywhere people do.

No one knows how many mosquitoes there are. So far, over twenty-five hundred different kinds have been identified and named.

We know about mosquitoes because they like to bite people and animals. Only the female will bite a living creature. One type goes only after human blood. Another bites only animals. A third prefers blood from birds.

The male mosquito never sucks blood. He has the same mouth as the female but would rather get food from plants.

When a female bites a human, she sticks a tube into the skin to suck up the blood. When the tube pierces the skin, it first shoots a juice into the body. This stops the blood from getting sticky and causes it to come out more quickly. The juice is what makes the mosquito bite itch so badly.

This same juice often carries diseases. In some countries, large numbers of people have died from malaria and yellow fever, which are carried by the mosquito. But do not fear—the diseases are under control in the United States and many other nations.

The female mosquito needs blood for her eggs. The blood helps the eggs grow and become stronger.

Mosquitoes multiply near water. Most of them lay their eggs in areas where there are many plants and weeds. Some will select a still body of water, like a pond or lake. Others enjoy the shore of a fast-moving stream. If there are no plants around, empty cans or old tires will do as well.

Mosquitoes go through four stages of growth: the egg, larva, pupa, and adult. The first three stages take place almost entirely in or near water. The adult stage is spent in the air.

Probably the most well-known feature of mosquitoes is their bite. Often they land on the back of the arm or leg, where it is hard to see them.

Sometimes people are like mosquitoes. We say unkind and cruel things behind someone's back. It is a mean habit, and many of us do it. The Bible calls this backbiting. When people aren't around, we talk about them. Often we do far more harm than a mosquito.

We don't like it when people gossip about us. The best example we can set is to refuse to say bad things about others.

I do this because I am afraid that when I come, you will not be what I want you to be. And I am afraid that I will not be what you want me to be. I am afraid that among you there may be arguing, jealousy, anger, selfish fighting, evil talk, gossip, pride, and confusion.

2 Corinthians 12:20 (ICB)

---

1. How many different kinds of mosquitoes are there?
2. How many stages do they go through?
3. Do we gossip about people? How can we set a better example of a Christian?

THERE ARE SO MANY KIND THINGS TO SAY. HELP US TO SAY THEM.

49
THE LIZARD FAMILY

Lizards have some of the strangest habits in all of nature. They come in different colors and sizes. Their lifestyle is often amazing.

One good example is the horned toad. Despite its name, it really is a lizard. These lizards are harmless, and children enjoy catching them. One type of horned toad has an ugly habit. When excited or angry, it can shoot a line of blood out of its eye. A couple of squirts of this, and most people will put it down.

The horned toad has a relative called the collared lizard, which has four legs but doesn't always use all of them. When the collared lizard is in a big hurry, it rises up on its back two legs and runs at top speed. It looks like a bike "popping a wheelie." Its name comes from the black marks on its neck that look like a collar.

The chuckwalla is the largest North American lizard. It measures up to fifteen inches long. Like most lizards, this one has its own means of defense. It normally hides among rocks. If an enemy attempts to pull it out, the chuckwalla enlarges its lungs. This "balloon" is then too big to pull out of its hole. In most cases the enemy gives up and leaves.

Usually, lizards are quiet creatures. The colorful gecko lizard is the oddball. It earns its name by saying something that sounds like "gecko, gecko."

No lizard is more bewildering than the skink. Some types of skink have a tail that looks like the head. A hawk will dive thinking it is aiming at

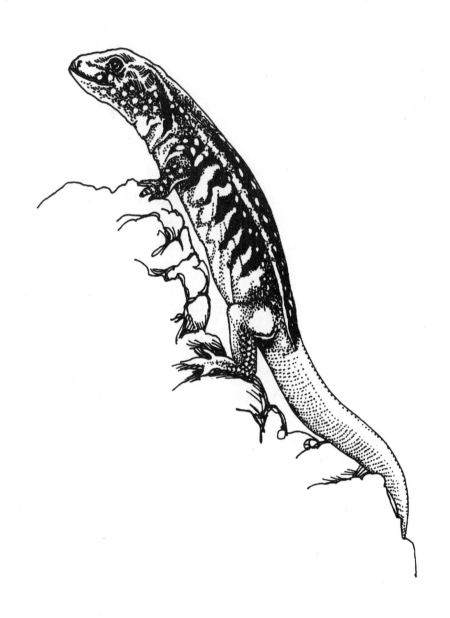

the lizard's head. Suddenly, the skink will run in the opposite direction.

An anole (pronounced *ah-KNOW-lee*) has still another odd ability. If an enemy grabs the anole by the tail, this lizard can simply disconnect it. The unhappy villain is left disappointed.

Many children buy lizards for pets. Unless special instructions are given, most of them die. Some have to be fed in a special way, and often they need a controlled temperature.

One of the lizards sold is the anole, commonly called the chameleon. These are popular because under certain situations they are able to turn colors. They can be green or brown, depending on their surroundings. Usually, temperature and fear determine their ability to change colors.

We aren't lizards, but someday Christians will change also. Our spirits will leave this earth and go into the presence of God. Then when Christ returns and raises the dead, our bodies will be changed—in a much greater way than the chameleon. We don't know what the change will be like, but it will be real.

In a moment, in the twinkling of an eye, at the last
trump: for the trumpet shall sound, and
the dead shall be raised incorruptible,
and we shall be changed.
1 Corinthians 15:52 (KJV)

---

1. How does the horned toad fight back?
2. How does a chuckwalla protect itself?
3. When will our bodies be changed?

EVERY PART OF OUR BODY WILL WORK WELL WHEN WE MEET JESUS CHRIST IN HEAVEN.

50

Almost Like Us

Chimpanzees act a great deal like humans. When chimps grow old, they even get bald. They are easy to tame and have excellent memories. Like happy children, chimpanzees are extremely curious and excitable.

Even when it comes to colors, this animal seems to rise above the vision of other animals. Most creatures can see life in only a few shades of gray. The chimp sees a large choice of bright reds, greens, and yellows.

The female generally gives birth to one baby at a time. Her youngster will often stay at her side for as many as five years. Just like a human child, it loves to play games. Young chimps collect pieces of fruit and use them as toys.

When chimpanzees are old enough, they go out in search of food. This hunt may take them far from home. However, they enjoy their group, or large family, and return to it.

Most of the time chimps are looking for tasty leaves or fresh fruit. Once in a while they stop to eat a delicious bug.

If you want to see a chimpanzee out of a zoo, you will probably have to travel to Central or Western Africa. There they live in the rain forests, where they spend most of their time in the trees.

Some people even think chimps look a little like us. They grow to five feet tall and weigh 180 pounds. Their faces are similar to humans. They show moods and emotions. When they get excited, chimps let out a loud, hooting cry.

Chimps are hairy creatures. Their bodies are almost entirely covered. A chimp's hands might be black or pink.

A chimpanzee's arms and legs look like they are backward. It has long, powerful arms that seem to hang to the ground. Its legs are short and heavy. Most of the time a chimp walks on all four limbs, but sometimes it can stand up almost like a person.

This animal can't talk, but it can get its message across. Often they communicate by touching each other or by making signs with their hands.

If we were to make a list, we would see how much chimpanzees are like people. It is also interesting to see how different they are from us. A chimp can't do homework, cook a meal, or fix a bicycle.

The same thing happens when some people are "almost Christians." They are kind, helpful, and polite, but that doesn't make them Christians. In some ways they look like one, but there is still a big difference.

Christians are people who trust Jesus Christ. They know Christ died for their sins. And they ask for forgiveness and cleansing.

For ye are all the children of God
by faith in Christ Jesus.

Galatians 3:26 (KJV)

---

1. What do chimpanzees eat?

2. How are chimps like people?

3. How does someone become a Christian?

THANKS FOR INVITING US TO BECOME THE CHILDREN OF GOD.

51

SUNKEN TREASURES

In 1692, nature shook the ground and dumped an entire city into the sea. On June 7, at 11:43 A.M., an earthquake hit Port Royal, Jamaica. A huge tidal wave brought tons of water on top of the town. Within thirty minutes the town was sitting on the bottom of the sea.

Sometimes nature gets out of control, and instead of helping humans, it hurts them. Two thousand people died in half an hour. It was one of the few cases in history where a city was thrown into the ocean all at once.

The city sunken under the sea has fascinated scientists. Divers have gone down and brought back gold, silver, bottles, cannons, and pipes.

One of the most interesting things recovered was an old watch. When they investigated it closely, scientists saw that the hands had stopped at 11:43, the time of the earthquake.

Finding sunken treasure is a dangerous and expensive operation. But still many people are looking for ships that went down years ago. In some places they can buy maps that show where ships probably are submerged.

Dr. Harold Edgerton, who grew up on the flat land of Aurora, Nebraska, helped greatly in underwater search. Dr. Edgerton invented a scanning sonar. When this is moved across the bottom of the sea, it will tell the operator if there is something buried beneath the sand and mud.

Amazing wrecks are still being found. In 1960, Peter Throckmorton discovered a ship under eighty-five feet of water. The ship dated back to one thousand years before Christ. The date of the vessel was on the coins it was carrying.

Every once in a while sunken treasure is brought up in an unusual way. One group of busy treasure hunters are the fish that live there. They often swallow license plates, boots, watches, or silver cups.

More important treasures than these are in the sea. Today a large number of submarines are moving beneath the surface. Once in a great while one gets stuck and can't come up. The navy is busy making ships that will go under the sea and rescue submarine crews.

This is a dangerous job because of the pressure under the sea. They are getting better at it and will save many lives.

The ocean is so large and deep that it must hold many treasures long ago lost and forgotten.

One of the writers of the Bible wanted us to know God forgives our sins. He said it is just as if God threw our sins into the ocean. They are gone and forgotten. Speaking about God, he said:

You will tread our sins beneath your feet; you will throw them into the depths of the ocean!

Micah 7:19 (TLB)

1. What happened to Port Royal?
2. What did Dr. Edgerton invent?
3. Why does the Bible compare our sins to the ocean?

THANKS FOR THROWING AWAY OUR SINS AND FORGETTING THEM.

52

THE UNDERGROUND MOLE

Every person who has ever played in the dirt remembers how much fun it is to dig tunnels. Some of us made holes with our sticks and pretended they were homes. We made garages to park our small cars.

A chubby little creature called the mole does the same thing, but it isn't playing games. The mole spends almost all its life under the soft earth.

If a mole happens to come above ground for a few minutes, it is practically lost. The mole has tiny eyes and can barely see at all. Most of its life, the mole doesn't have to see.

These diggers are especially built for earth moving. Their faces come to a point to help push through the ground. Their two front feet are extra large, for power. Completely covered, moles are actually swimming through the ground.

We don't often see moles, but it is easy to find their work. A new lawn or sandy area may have a long snake-shaped bump in it. Very likely, a mole has been traveling through it.

Moles seem to enjoy snow. They can move rapidly through the soft, cold flakes. The light and easy movement must feel particularly good to them.

While the mole digs through the ground, it is always looking for something to eat. Earthworms are especially tasty. Ants make an excellent dinner. Sometimes even a lizard is a tasty choice.

In March and April, baby moles are born. In America, moles usually build nests a foot or more underground. The babies are placed there until they are able to start digging for themselves.

The moles' relatives in Australia are just a little different. They have pouches for their babies, like kangaroos. The young moles hold on inside and feed from their mothers.

If you are careful, you might be able to watch a mole work. When you see a lumpy tunnel on the ground, stand back a fair distance and look at it move. Don't get too close or the mole will feel your steps. When it does, it starts backing up as quickly as possible, using its tail as a guide.

During the days of the prophet Isaiah, some people owned little statues and pretended they were tiny gods. They would worship the statues, called idols, by bowing in front of them, praying to them, and offering burned grass or leaves. Isaiah said when we realize who the true God is, we can throw away the old statues. We can take them out and bury them and let the moles play with them.

Statues, or idols, cannot hear or see or help us in any way. But our God is alive.

Then at last they will abandon their gold and
silver idols to the moles and bats.

Isaiah 2:20 (TLB)

1. Describe a mole's eyes.
2. What do moles eat?
3. Why is it useless to worship statues?

WE HAVE A GREAT GOD WHO DOESN'T LIVE IN LITTLE STATUES OR IN THE GROUND LIKE A MOLE.

53

WILD DOGS

Dogs are some of the most popular animals in the world. They appear in a wide variety of breeds, from a gentle French poodle to the highly dangerous dhole (pronounced *dole*).

Some of the meanest dogs in the world are the Cape hunting dogs of South Africa. They even look cruel. A few times they have been tamed as pups, but as they grow older they usually get wild.

Cape dogs hunt in groups called packs. There might be as few as four, but there can be sixty in a pack. There is nothing they are afraid to attack. They can travel long distances just to capture an antelope and eat it.

They are greedy dogs and are continuously searching for food. The Cape dogs' hunting abilities are excellent. They can work in harmony to outsmart a victim. A few of the dogs might run ahead to cut off the path of an animal. Others will hurry alongside in case the victim tries to cut back. Then, as if well trained, the dogs will strike.

Cape hunters will have as many as twelve pups at a time. They build nests in the ground and live close to each other in colonies.

Dhole dogs are just as vicious. They live mostly in Russia, Korea, and Java. Like Cape hunters, they travel in packs. The stories of their fearlessness are often told. The dhole has attacked bears, and some believe this group has even killed tigers.

One of the strangest members of the dog family is the dingo, which lives in Australia. Dingoes look like dogs you might find in your neighborhood except for their pointed ears that refuse to lie down.

The natives who live in the bush may use dingoes as hunting dogs. But they aren't very good at it because many dingoes will run away the first chance they get.

The dingo is a dog without a bark. It can yelp or howl but cannot make a regular dog sound.

This dog is hated and hunted constantly. Farmers especially dislike dingoes because of the destruction they cause. Dingoes will attack sheep that they have no intention of eating. Their real problem is just greediness. The dingo wants more than it can use.

Most of us are like the dingo. Children and adults see so many things they would like to have. We spend a great deal of time getting things we can't really use. This is what greediness is. The person who learns to share has begun to fight greed.

And they are as greedy dogs, never satisfied.

Isaiah 56:11 (TLB)

1. How do Cape hunters work together?
2. What does the dhole dog attack?
3. Name one way in which we could share with others.

THANKS FOR SHARING YOUR ONLY SON WITH US.

54

THE WASP STING

"Wipe the mud off your feet." Every child has heard this. Even adults sometimes forget and track mud into the house. Sometimes mud can only be called a mess, but other times it's great fun.

Some children enjoy making pies or building little roads for toy cars. Older boys like to ride their dirt bikes and watch the mud spin off their wheels.

A certain type of wasp has enjoyed playing in the mud ever since it was an infant. In fact, the mud dauber wasp was born in dried mud. That is what its home was made of, and that is where its eggs were laid.

Mud daubers' homes can be seen on the roofs of old barns. Sometimes they are attached to the ceiling of an attic in a tall home.

The food of a mud dauber isn't anything special. It usually consists of fresh spider. The mother is the chief hunter. She swings down on the prey and stings it. The spider is paralyzed and easily carried back to the mud home. When the baby wasps break out of their eggs, they find a delicious supper stuck to their wall.

But mud daubers aren't the only wasps. Potter wasps don't make their homes out of dull mud. They carefully mix clay. The adult carries each tiny piece and attaches it to a tree branch. When the potter wasp is finished, it has a first-class home. Wind and rain have a tough time hurting this home.

Potter wasps would rather have fresh caterpillar for dinner than spiders. Young beetles also make a good meal.

This wasp looks dangerous to man but is really our friend. They eat insects that normally destroy fruit and vegetables.

The Potter wasp likes to pack its food on the walls of its home, also. When its egg and a caterpillar are placed neatly inside, the nest is sealed tightly. The new wasp develops inside its cell until it's strong enough to break out.

Don't look for every wasp nest on a ceiling or in a tree. The famous killer wasp makes its home in the ground. A full inch in length, it isn't afraid of its much larger enemies. In July and August, killer wasps attack the huge cicada.

Usually, the killer wasp can't carry the cicada far. It may start off flying with the huge victim, but soon the wasp has to hit the ground. Strong and tough, the wasp then drags its supper across the grass. It then pushes the helpless cicada into its nest.

This isn't the end of our search for wasp homes. One species of wasp lives inside a tree. The carpenter wasp can dig three or four inches into solid wood. Like its relatives, it also uses mud inside its home.

The stinger plays an important part in the wasp's life. Without it, wasps would be fairly harmless.

Almost everyone gets stung by a wasp or bee sooner or later. These stings can be terribly painful. Some people even become sick from a wasp sting.

One of the hardest things we face is the death of a friend or relative. But the Bible says God sent Jesus Christ to help us. By giving us a place in heaven, He took the big sting out of death.

O death, where then your victory? Where then your sting?

1 Corinthians 15:55 (TLB)

1. How does a mud dauber wasp capture its food?
2. Where does a carpenter wasp live?
3. How does Jesus Christ change death?

BECAUSE CHRIST IS ALIVE, I CAN LIVE WITH HIM IN HEAVEN.

55

THE FASTEST ANIMAL

The fastest animal on foot is the cheetah. It has been timed running at seventy miles an hour. After it runs a quarter of a mile, its speed cuts down considerably. But during that first sprint, nothing can outrun it.

To understand its speed, try this example: The next time you are in a car, ask the driver to tell you when the car gets to fifty-five miles per hour. When the automobile is going that fast, look out the window and imagine a cheetah passing the car. That is exactly what they can do.

Cheetahs can be terrible killers. They can also be tamed and have been kept as pets. The princess of India used to have them trained for hunting. Even as grown animals, cheetahs can be taught to obey commands.

Hoods are put on their heads until they arrive at the chosen fields. When the hood is removed, the cheetah will take off after its prey. It will then return to its trainer.

Cheetahs have beautiful black spots and are often confused with leopards. They have to be taught by their parents to hunt and kill. If taken as young cubs, cheetahs are not natural killers.

Despite its excellent speed, the cheetah prefers to use its head. A quiet hunter, it will try to sneak up on its victim. It glides slowly through the jungles until it is close to the animal. Then, without warning, it makes its move. Seldom does anything get away.

In some ways cheetahs are more like dogs than cats. They have long legs, a small head, and a call that sounds like a dog's. They are the only members of the cat family that can't draw in their claws.

Cheetahs prefer to eat antelope, gazelle, and other grazing animals. Usually, they hunt in pairs or family groups.

There isn't much chance of a cheetah chasing most of us. (It wouldn't do any good to run; you might try hiding.) Cheetahs are found in Africa and India. Long ago they lived north of Israel, in Syria and Persia.

One of the happiest parts of being young is the ability to run. Those who are healthy enough can feel the breeze pushing through their hair. Your legs can help you race, and sometimes you can imagine you are a cheetah.

Running is great for games. It comes in handy if you need to go for help. Some young people use running to get into trouble and try to get away.

One of the writers of the Bible thought about speed and about God. Wouldn't it be great if we were in a hurry to follow Jesus Christ, as if we could hardly wait to be like Him?

The Lord is a strong fortress. The godly run to him and are safe.

Proverbs 18:10 (TLB)

1. How fast do cheetahs run?
2. What do they eat?
3. Who should we run after?

WE ARE IN A HURRY FOR MOST THINGS. HELP US RUN TO FOLLOW YOU.

56

HATCHING EGGS

Every once in a while I see little blue-speckled eggs in my backyard. These are robin eggs that were blown out of their nests.

Do you ever wonder what a bird has to do to hatch a chick? It isn't easy, but the parent knows exactly how to handle the situation.

A bird controls the hatching by controlling the temperature of the eggs. Many eggs need a steady temperature of around ninety-nine degrees (about thirty-seven degrees Celsius). Mother birds keep this warmth by sitting on the eggs and getting off at the right times.

If it is a hot day, a bird might spend only twenty minutes each hour on the eggs. When the night gets chilly, a robin may sit on the eggs all night.

We usually think of a mother bird sitting on her eggs. This is only partly true. With some types, the father and mother take turns. A few species are accustomed to having only the father sit on the eggs.

The whole process becomes more tricky because of the need for food. Someone has to go "shopping" and at the same time not leave for too long.

Birds have bare patches underneath them to give warmth and control the temperature of the nest. If necessary, they can push their bodies harder against the egg to give it more heat. The object is to get the egg warm through to its center. It takes around two weeks for most birds to hatch. Some birds need a certain number of eggs before they start holding the temperature. One type needs two eggs, another may need four.

There are nine thousand different species, or types, of birds. Each kind lays an egg like no other. A robin egg doesn't look like an ostrich egg. A sparrow's egg won't look like a pigeon's. The color, shape, size, or other marks will distinguish one from another.

Eggs are normally laid during the morning.

The differences in sizes are amazing. The huge ostrich lays a two-pound egg. The tiny hummingbird lays the smallest dot.

When the big day comes, the new bird has to do the major portion of the work. Chicks use their young beaks to break open the shell. Some take a few hours, while others take several days.

A mother bird goes to a lot of trouble to lay the eggs and hatch them. Now she will search for food to keep her chicks alive. She usually has no interest in stealing anyone else's chicks but is happy with her own.

People who steal from others are just like birds with another bird's chicks—they soon lose interest and don't take care of them. The person who works for what she gets feels good about it and takes better care of it. Stealing is an ugly way to live and a habit that hurts everyone.

Like a bird that fills her nest with young she has not hatched and which will soon desert her and fly away, so is the man who gets his wealth by unjust means. Sooner or later he will lose his riches and at the end of his life become a poor old fool.

Jeremiah 17:11 (TLB)

1. What temperature is necessary for most eggs?
2. How long is it before many eggs hatch?
3. What do we think about things we steal?

STEALING HURTS EVERYONE.

57

DEEP-SEA DIVER

One of the South Pole's most interesting animals is the Weddell seal. This huge deep-sea diver can weigh up to nine hundred pounds and swims like a minnow.

People may wish they could do what this creature can. This seal can stop breathing for thirty minutes while looking for food. It can dive fifteen hundred feet and catch most fish, including the squid. Some Weddell seals have stayed underwater for forty-five minutes. Humans can't begin to do this.

The secret to such long dives is the seal's ability to change its heartbeat. Normally, its heartbeat is 150 times per minute. When the seal dives, it lowers its heartbeat to ten beats a minute. A human would get bubbles in his blood diving this deep. The Weddell seal merely lives off the air in its body.

These seals are born to be fat. They weigh a plump sixty pounds when they are born. In two weeks of feeding on the mother's butterfat milk, junior will increase to 120 pounds. It is a hard job for the mother. While she is feeding a baby seal, she will lose up to three hundred pounds.

A mother Weddell means well but isn't terribly intelligent. For some reason she gets confused at the sight of danger. If an animal or human comes near her, she will start killing her young pups. She doesn't seem to understand what she has done. For days the mother stays with her children, even after they are dead.

The seal enjoys ice. In the coldest season it will dig a hole and live under the ice. The seal uses its teeth to make holes for air. When it grows older, the Weddell seal has badly worn teeth.

In old age the seal looks for a place to retire. It heads for the top of a mountain. Weddell seals have been found thirty-five miles from shore and three thousand feet above sea level. If a young seal is sick or wounded, it heads for the mountains. When it gets better it will return. This gives the seal a chance to get away from a tough life, but it can still enjoy the cold snow and ice.

When we travel to the farthest ends of the earth, the proof of God's work is exciting. The beautiful sunsets, the pure air, the amazing life of little-known creatures are all part of His handiwork. It is a land that richly displays the skillful hand of God.

The psalmist had never been to the Poles, but he would have found God there as easily as in the Garden of Eden, and he never doubted it.

He quiets the raging oceans and all the world's clamor. In the farthest corners of the earth the glorious acts of God shall startle everyone. The dawn and sunset shout for joy!

Psalm 65:7–8 (TLB)

1. Why can seals dive so deep?
2. Where do they go to retire?
3. Name two things you think are beatuiful in nature.

THANKS FOR MAKING THE EARTH SO INTERESTING.

58

THE FRIENDLESS SKUNK

If we see a small black-and-white animal coming our way, we had better move. It may look lovable and soft, but don't be fooled. Skunks give off a terrible odor.

When they feel frightened, this member of the weasel family has a powerful weapon. It merely turns around, picks up its tail—and look out! Skunks can shoot a spray for ten to fifteen feet.

The smell is so strong it sometimes bothers people a mile away. Often, any clothes in contact with the spray will have to be destroyed. The skunk's weapon is too powerful to take lightly. This explains why few animals even try to attack this unhurried creature.

For some reason, skunks live only in the Americas. This includes North America, Mexico, and South America.

The skunk's color seems to work differently for him than the color of other animals. Some animals are green or brown so that they can hide in the forest. Not the skunk. It is black-and-white—and stands out like spilled grape juice on a rug! The skunk's plan of defense is to be seen. If other animals can just see it coming, they are happy to move out.

This holds true until we come to humans. People hunt skunks for their fur. Some eat skunk meat and say it tastes great.

Often false rumors are spread about skunks. They actually are clean animals. They give off their odor only when afraid. Most skunks do not carry rabies. The few who do, get it from the bite of another animal.

Many skunks prefer night work. The day is an inviting time to sleep. When they do go out, skunks are usually in search of a good meal. Dinner might consist of a few worms, possibly some bird eggs, maybe a side order of insects. A rat or a mouse would really top off a skunk's evening meal.

Baby skunks are called *kittens*. A healthy mother will have four to six each year.

Skunks can fool us. After they give off their odor, some people think it is safe to go near them. These people are usually sorry. Skunks save a second shot for those who are unwise.

No matter how much some people know, they still do foolish things. Adults and children often hurt themselves, doing something they know is dangerous. The smart person listens to good warnings—and obeys them.

Don't waste your breath on a rebel. He will
despise the wisest advice.

Proverbs 23:9 (TLB)

---

1. How far away can the skunk odor be sensed?
2. How does a skunk's color help him?
3. What should we do with good warnings?

WE CAN PREVENT A LOT OF PAIN BY LISTENING TO GOOD ADVICE.

59

THE JUNGLE IN YOUR YARD

Not all of us have flown off to a thick, scary jungle where lots of fascinating animals live. Someday we might travel to see lions in the wild or howler monkeys racing through the trees or multicolored birds calling in the distance. We can't go now, but maybe later we will be able.

For now we might be happy to take a trip to visit the jungle just outside our door. We are talking about that mysterious place we call our lawn or our yard, where many kinds of amazing creatures live.

Spiders, snakes, wasps, mice, flies, worms, and other creepy things either live in the grass and weeds or they come to visit. Some dart around during the daytime, while others scurry around in the dark.

Insects lead a particularly dangerous existence living on a lawn. People might step on them. Children might collect them and put them in a jar. Snakes could eat them for dinner. Birds might sweep down and gobble them up.

Even flies have to watch out. They might land to lay eggs in the grass as gently as possible. But when they turn to take off, the unsuspecting pilot might crash into a spider's web and not be able to escape.

For the fun of it, take a paper and pencil and lie on the lawn on your belly. Lying still, you will be able to see a wide array of neat creatures making their way around. Some are tiny. Some are large. One moves slowly. The other is scurrying around. One might be chasing something. Another might be running away.

Unfortunately, we think the best parts of nature are in a far-off country. Actually, an entire jungle exists only a few feet outside the front door.

God made a wide variety of creatures. Some fly across the sky like airplanes. Others race across the earth fast as a car. Some are large enough to knock down a small house. Others are small enough to crawl inside our windows even when our windows are closed.

A quick trip to our front lawn or to the empty lot in the neighborhood could help us appreciate how wonderful God is. Watching crawling things in the grass could give us reason to worship God.

How many are your works, O Lord! In wisdom
you made them all; the earth is full of your
creatures.

Psalm 104:24 (NIV)

1. Name three things that live on your lawn.
2. Have you ever seen a spider on your lawn? What color was it?
3. Do you ever thank God for creating so many interesting things?

OPEN MY EYES TO SEE MORE OF THE WONDERS YOU HAVE MADE.

60

JUMPING KANGAROOS

Let's learn a new word today. The word is *marsupial* (pronounced *mar-SOUP-ial*). If we say it over a few times, it will become easy to remember.

A small number of animals have pouches on their abdomens to carry their babies. The pouch looks like a purse or a bag. Wombats, opossums, some moles, and kangaroos are the most well-known marsupials.

Kangaroos live in Australia and New Zealand. Many are as small as kittens, but others can be seven feet tall and weigh over two hundred pounds. Don't let the size of a kangaroo fool you. The great gray variety can run twenty-five miles an hour and have been known to jump twenty-six feet. They have no trouble bounding over a six-foot fence and could even clear a ten-foot one!

Not every kangaroo enjoys the ground. Tree kangaroos prefer to jump from branch to branch. They aren't quite two feet long and use their long tails to keep their balance. They can leap thirty feet to the ground without any apparent harm.

One kangaroo you might want to be careful around is the rat kangaroo. They seem to be more like skunks than anything else. If they become excited, rat 'roos can let off a terrible odor. Their numbers are decreasing in Australia. They are actually a cute animal. The rat kangaroo can carry bundles of grass with its curved tail while it moves on all four legs.

The kangaroos most of us see in zoos are usually wallabies. They have

large feet and are gray, red, or brown.

Great gray kangaroos are the largest variety, but they start out tiny. Newborn babies are only the size of a quarter. The baby crawls immediately into its mother's pouch. There it can feed comfortably from the mother's body for the next five or six months. During the entire time it might never poke its head out.

Slowly the baby begins to get adventurous. For a couple of weeks the infant will poke its head out and look the world over. Then one day it takes the big plunge and jumps out.

The kangaroo still doesn't forget the warm protection of its mother. For a few more weeks the youngster will jump back into the pouch if it gets hungry or afraid.

Mother kangaroos mean a great deal to their young. They look up to her as the strong and helpful one when they need something.

Most of us really enjoy our mothers. They have done so many kind and loving things for us. We wouldn't do anything to hurt her. That is why so many children are extra careful not to get into trouble. They have a wonderful mother, and they want her to be proud of them.

Happy is the man with a level-headed son; sad the
mother of a rebel.

Proverbs 10:1 (TLB)

1. What is a marsupial?
2. How big is the largest kangaroo?
3. Name one thing you could do today to make your mother happy.

THANK GOD FOR MY MOTHER.